Keep Your Eyes On the Horizon:
Business Lessons from Unsinkable Titanic

By: Ade Asefeso, Steffen Brygger Lund & Hadrian Parry

Copyright 2014 by:
Ade Asefeso, Steffen Brygger Lund & Hadrian Parry.
All rights reserved.

ISBN-13: 978-1500690809

ISBN-10: 1500690805

Publisher: AA Global Sourcing Ltd
Website: http://www.aaglobalsourcing.com

Table of Contents

Preface 5
Disclaimer 7
Dedication 8
Chapter 1: Introduction 9
Chapter 2: Keep Your Eyes On the Horizon 15
Chapter 3: Why Some Leaders Failed to Keep their Eyes On the Horizon 19
Chapter 4: Sometimes Leaders Can't See What is Right in Front of Them 27
Chapter 5: Leadership Failures Sank the Unsinkable 31
Chapter 6: Big Company Bureaucracy 39
Chapter 7: Some Organizations' Culture is Like the Titanic 53
Chapter 8: Project Management Lessons from the Titanic Disaster 63
Chapter 9: Disaster Prevention Lessons Learned from the Titanic 73
Chapter 10: Image and Decision Making 83
Chapter 11: Crisis Management Lessons from the Titanic 89
Chapter 12: Crisis Leadership/Business Continuity Lessons 97
Chapter 13: Business Contingency Planning 103
Chapter 14: Managing Multicultural Teams 109
Chapter 15: Lessons from Lehman Brothers 117

Chapter 16: Three Traps That Make the Glory Days Fleeting 127
Chapter 17: Accountability 135
Chapter 18: Lessons for Modern Business Leaders 145
Chapter 19: Managing People on a Sinking Ship 149
Chapter 20: Critical Threats that May Sink Your Business 157
Chapter 21: Turning the Titanic 161
Chapter 22: How Small Businesses Can Keep Their Ship from Sinking 167
Chapter 23: Ways to Save Your Sinking Company 177
Chapter 24: When the Ship is Sinking 183
Chapter 25: Unsung Heroes of Business World . 189
Chapter 26: Concluding the Journey 193
Other Book from the same Authors 199

Preface

In our first book **"The Emperor's New Clothes: A Contemporary Business Life Edition,"** we drew parallels between the characters, motifs, and moral of the famous fairy-tale by Hans Christian Andersen and today's business world. Our readers were encouraged to recognize the "Emperor," "Weaver," "Child" and "Father" in themselves. This first book of ours encouraged business practitioners to find the courage to speak up when they see "nakedness" in any proposed business initiative.

While preparing for our first book we often heard people talking about renowned and glorious corporations that "went down like the unsinkable Titanic" and the idea for this book slowly emerged. Titanic hit an iceberg on the night of April 14, 1912 and sank in just over two-and-a-half hours later.

During our study of the Titanic catastrophe it became clear to us that the leadership lessons from the Titanic clearly apply to businesses today as much as they did to the ships at this iconic event more than 100 years ago.

This book will draw parallels between the Titanic catastrophe and today's contemporary business world. As our reader will hopefully see, there are many lessons to be learned by today's business practitioners.

We dedicate our book to the "corporate sailors that keep their ships afloat". Keeping their companies healthy and afloat was and still is the name of the game for the leaders in today's contemporary and ever changing business world.

Disclaimer

This publication is designed to provide competent and reliable information regarding the subject matter covered. However, it is sold with the understanding that the authors and publisher are not engaged in rendering professional advice. The authors and publishers specifically disclaim any liability that is incurred from the use or application of contents of this book.

If you purchased this book without a cover you should be aware that this book may have been stolen property and reported as "unsold and destroyed" to the publisher. In this case neither the authors nor the publisher has received any payment for this "stripped book."

Dedication

To the corporate sailors that keep their ships afloat!

Chapter 1: Introduction

You may already know that the Titanic hit an iceberg at 11:40 p.m. on the night of April 14, 1912 and sunk just over two-and-a-half hours later, but do you know the following facts about the Titanic?

1. Cancelled Lifeboat Drill

Originally, a lifeboat drill was scheduled to take place on board the Titanic on April 14, 1912 - the day the Titanic hit the iceberg however, for an unknown reason, Captain Smith cancelled the drill. Many believe that had the drill taken place, more lives could have been saved.

2. Only Seconds

From the time the lookouts sounded the alert, the officers on the bridge had only 37 seconds to react before the Titanic hit the iceberg. In that time, First Officer Murdoch ordered "hard a-starboard" (which turned the ship to port - left). He also ordered the engine room to put the engines in reverse. The Titanic did bank left, but it wasn't quite enough.

3. The Titanic's Newspaper

The Titanic seemed to have everything on board, including its own newspaper. The Atlantic Daily Bulletin was printed every day on board the Titanic. The newspaper included news, advertisements, stock prices, horse-racing results, society gossip, and the day's menu.

4. Lifeboats Not Full

Not only were there not enough lifeboats to save everyone on board, most of the lifeboats that were launched off the Titanic were not filled to capacity. For instance, the first lifeboat to launch, Lifeboat 7 from the starboard side only carried 24 people, despite having a capacity of 65 (two additional people later transferred to Lifeboat 7 from Lifeboat 5). However, it was Lifeboat 1 that carried the fewest people - only seven crew and five passengers (a total of 12 people) despite having a capacity for 40.

5. Only Two Bathtubs

Although most passengers had to share bathrooms (only the two promenade suites in first class had private bathrooms), third class had it rough with only two bathtubs for more than 700 passengers.

6. Another Boat Was Closer for Rescue

When the Titanic began sending out distress signals, the Californian, rather than the Carpathia, was the closest ship; yet the Californian did not respond until it was much too late to help. At 12:45 a.m. on April 15, 1912, crew members on the Californian saw mysterious lights in the sky (the distress flares sent up from the Titanic) and woke up their captain to tell him about it. Unfortunately, the captain issued no orders. Since the ship's wireless operator had already gone to bed, the Californian was unaware of any distress signals from the Titanic until the morning, but by then the Carpathia had already picked up all the survivors. Many people believe that if the Californian had responded to the Titanic's pleas for help, many more lives could have been saved.

7. Two Dogs Rescued

With the order for women and children first into the lifeboats, plus the knowledge that there were not enough lifeboats for everyone on board the Titanic to be saved, it is a bit surprising that two dogs made it into the lifeboats. Of the nine dogs on board the Titanic, the two that were rescued were a Pomeranian and a Pekinese.

8. The Fourth Funnel

In what is now an iconic image, the side view of the Titanic clearly shows four cream and black funnels. While three of these released the steam from the boilers, the fourth was just for show. The designers thought the ship would look more impressive with four funnels rather than three.

9. A Royal Mail Ship

The R.M.S. Titanic was a Royal Mail Ship, a designation which meant the Titanic was officially responsible for delivering mail for the British postal service. On board the Titanic was a Sea Post Office with five mail clerks (two British and three American). These mail clerks were responsible for the 3,423 sacks of mail (seven million individual pieces of mail) on board the Titanic. Interestingly, although no mail has yet been recovered from the wreck of the Titanic, if it were, the U.S. Postal Service would still try to deliver it (the USPS because most of the mail was being sent to the United State of America).

10. Corpses Recovered

On April 17, 1912, the day before survivors of the Titanic disaster reached New York, the Mackay-Bennett was sent off from Halifax, Nova Scotia to search for bodies. On board the Mackay-Bennett were embalming supplies, 40 embalmers, tons of ice, and 100 coffins. Although the Mackay-Bennett found 306 bodies, 116 of these were too badly damaged to take all the way back to shore. Attempts were made to identify each body found. Additional ships were also sent out to look for bodies. In all, 328 bodies were found, but 119 of these were badly damaged and thus were buried at sea.

Over 100 years since the Titanic sank to the bottom of the ocean. 1,517 people died that night. They weren't killed by an iceberg; they died because of unrealistic self-confidence, complacency, arrogance and disorganization. Thus this resonates well with what you also see in today's corporate world; an ocean full of dangerous icebergs that will sink you and your business if you don't keep your eyes on the horizon.

Chapter 2: Keep Your Eyes On the Horizon

Every Organization is blessed with excellent value based people who are able to set strategy and goals for the company, analyse the steps that will be required to deliver that strategy and goal; have confidence to take those steps, diligently work through the associated issues that arise while those steps are taken and finally to visualize the steps to be taken as company strategy evolves.

A creative attitude is a fuel of progress and growth. Either you will find a way or you will make one.

It can be done but will it be done? That's entirely up to you. Our experience tells us that there are 9

important prerequisites for making things happen successfully.
1. When you can see it yourself doing it, it can be done.

2. When you are committed, it can be done.

3. When you can envision it, it can be done.

4. When the entire world says you can't and yet you still believe, it can be done.

5. When you keep your eyes on the goal, it can be done.

6. When you find a reason, deep within yourself, it can be done.

7. When you truly want it, it can be done.

8. When you develop a step-by step plan, it can be done.

9. When you stay focussed, it can be done.

When you know "you can", it can be done. Even when obstacles stand in your way, it can be done.

We all live our lives in comfort zones; avoid risky situations and avoiding the potential to fail. But in order to get ahead of competition and master the ongoing change in our life, we must go out of our comfort zone and a can do approach would certainly lead us towards that. Creativity and being innovative are crucial capabilities for modern organizational effectiveness.

It is people with the right capabilities, who can transform an organization. At the same time it is very important to note that Success does not come merely by having capable people but by having capable and willing people. True capabilities of an organization are all about having people with required knowledge and skills along with a positive attitude and mindset. Positive attitude can be perceived through a "We Can Do It" behaviour. Often also what we call a "NIKE Attitude" helps a lot: JUST DO IT.

Leaders have a key role to play in building a positive attitude amongst people for which systematic efforts to create right mindset and provide the required skill set is a must. It is the responsibility of everyone in the organization to utilize the enablers provided by the leadership to enhance capabilities and with strong will develop the mindset-"WE CAN DO IT".

Organizations that encourage individual abilities and hold employees accountable for achieving goals are more likely to succeed.

Today's organizations operate in a very different environment. Volatility, uncertainty, complexity and ambiguity are constant realities in the 21st century.

"Team" means group of individuals working together to achieve common goals and it is the fuel that allows common people to attain uncommon results. Effective team work must have major characteristics like role clarity, effective communication, good leadership, clear vision, passion for work etc.

People who are great leaders tap the POTENTIAL of their people and make the Organization GREAT while constantly keeping their eyes on the horizon and avoiding potential icebergs.

Chapter 3: Why Some Leaders Failed to Keep their Eyes On the Horizon

Dominique Strauss-Kahn is just the latest in a string of high-profile leaders making the perp walk. What went wrong, and how can we learn from it?

To stay grounded executives must prepare themselves to confront enormous complexities and pressures.

Recently several high-level leaders have mysteriously lost their way. Dominique Strauss-Kahn, former head of the International Monetary Fund and a leading French politician, was arraigned on charges of sexual assault. Before that David Sokol, rumoured to be Warren Buffett's successor, was forced to resign for trading in Lubrizol stock prior to recommending that Berkshire Hathaway purchase the company.

Examples of other recent failures

1. Hewlett-Packard CEO Mark Hurd resigned for submitting false expense reports concerning his relationship with a contractor.
2. US Senator John Ensign (R-NV) resigned after covering up an extramarital affair with monetary payoffs.
3. Lee B. Farkas, former chairman of giant mortgage lender Taylor, Bean & Whitaker was found guilty for his role in one of the largest bank fraud schemes in American history.

These talented leaders were highly successful in their respective fields and at the peak of their careers. This makes their behaviour especially perplexing, raising questions about what caused them to lose their way.

1. Why do leaders known for integrity and leadership engage in unethical activities?

2. Why do they risk great careers and unblemished reputations for such ephemeral gains?

3. Do they think they won't get caught or do they believe their elevated status puts them above the law?

4. Was this the first time they did something inappropriate, or have they been on the slippery slope for years?

In these ongoing revelations, the media, politicians, and the general public frequently characterize these leaders as bad people, even calling them evil. Simplistic notions of good and bad only cloud our understanding of why good leaders lose their way, and how this could happen to any of us.

Leaders who lose their way are not necessarily bad people; rather, they lose their moral bearings, often yielding to seductions in their paths. Very few people go into leadership roles to cheat or do evil, yet we all have the capacity for actions we deeply regret unless we stay grounded.

Self-reflection: a path to leadership development

Before anyone takes on a leadership role, they should ask themselves, "Why do I want to lead?" and "What is the purpose of my leadership?" These questions are simple to ask, but finding the real answers may take decades. If the honest answers are power, prestige, and money, leaders are at risk of relying on external gratification for fulfilment. There is nothing wrong with desiring these outward symbols as long as they are combined with a deeper desire to serve something greater than oneself.

Leaders whose goal is the quest for power over others, unlimited wealth, or the fame that comes with success tend to look to others to gain satisfaction, and often appear self-centred and egotistical. They start to believe their own press. As leaders of institutions, they eventually believe the institution cannot succeed without them.

The leadership trap

While most people value fair compensation for their accomplishments, few leaders start out seeking only money, power, and prestige. Along the way, the rewards - bonus, newspaper articles, perks, and stock appreciation fuel increasing desires for more.

This creates a deep desire to keep it going, often driven by desires to overcome narcissistic wounds from childhood. Many times, this desire is so strong that leaders breach the ethical standards that previously governed their conduct, which can be bizarre and even illegal.

Very few people go into leadership to cheat or do evil

As Novartis chairman Daniel Vasella (HBS PMD 57) told Fortune magazine, "for many of us the idea of being a successful manager leading the company from peak to peak, delivering the goods quarter by quarter is an intoxicating one. It is a pattern of celebration leading to belief, leading to distortion. When you achieve good results… you are typically celebrated, and you begin to believe that the figure at the centre of all that champagne-toasting is yourself."

When leaders focus on external gratification instead of inner satisfaction, they lose their grounding. Often they reject the honest critic who speaks truth to power. Instead, they surround themselves with sycophants who tell them what they want to hear. Over time, they are unable to engage in honest dialogue; others after a while learn not to confront them with reality.

The dark side of leadership

Many leaders get to the top by imposing their will on others, even destroying people standing in their way. When they reach the top, they may be paranoid that others are trying to knock them off their pedestal. Sometimes they develop an impostor complex, caused by deep insecurities that they are not good enough and may be unmasked.

To prove they are not impostors, they drive so hard for perfection that they are incapable of acknowledging their failures. When confronted by them, they convince themselves and others that these problems are neither their fault nor their responsibility. Or they look for scapegoats to blame for their problems. Using their power, charisma, and communications skills, they force people to accept these distortions, causing entire organizations to lose touch with reality.

At this stage leaders are vulnerable to making big mistakes, such as violating the law or putting their organizations' existence at risk. Their distortions convince them they are doing nothing wrong, or they rationalize that their deviations are acceptable to achieve a greater good.

During the financial crisis, Lehman CEO Richard Fuld refused to recognize that Lehman was undercapitalized. His denial turned balance sheet miss-judgments into catastrophe for the entire financial system. Fuld persistently rejected advice to seek added capital, deluding himself into thinking the federal government would bail him out. When the crisis hit, he had run out of options other than bankruptcy.

It is lonely at the top, because leaders know they are ultimately responsible for the lives and fortunes of people. If they fail, many get deeply hurt. They often deny the burdens and loneliness, becoming incapable of facing reality. They shut down their inner voice, because it is too painful to confront or even acknowledge; it may, however, appear in their dreams as they try to resolve conflicts rustling around inside their heads.

Meanwhile, their work lives and personal lives get out of balance. They lose touch with those closest to them; their spouses, children, and best friends or co-opt them with their points of view. Eventually, they lose their capacity to think logically about important issues.

Values-centred leadership

Leading is high stress work. There is no way to avoid the constant challenges of being responsible for people, organizations, outcomes, and uncertainties in the environment. Leaders who move up have greater freedom to control their destinies, but also experience increased pressure and seduction.

Leaders can avoid these pitfalls by devoting themselves to personal development that cultivates their inner compass, or True North. This requires reframing their leadership from being heroes to being servants of the people they lead. In our mind true leadership is all about making good things happen through others. This process requires thought and introspection because many people get into leadership roles in response to their ego needs. It enables them to transition from seeking external gratification to finding internal satisfaction by making meaningful contributions through their leadership.

Maintaining their equilibrium amid this stress requires discipline. Some people practice meditation or yoga to relieve stress, while others find solace in prayer or taking long runs or walks. Still others find relief through laughter, music, television, sporting events, and reading. Their choices do not matter, as long as they relieve stress to enable them to think clearly about work and personal issues.

A system to support values-centred leadership

The reality is that people cannot stay grounded by themselves. Leaders depend on people closest to them to stay centred. They should seek out people who influence them in profound ways and stay connected to them. Often their spouse or partner knows them best. They aren't impressed by titles, prestige, or wealth accumulation; instead, they worry that these outward symbols may be causing the loss of authenticity.

Spouses and partners can't carry this entire burden though. We need mentors to advise us when facing difficult decisions. Reliable mentors are entirely honest and straight with us, defining reality and developing action plans.

As Senator Ensign told his fellow senators in a farewell speech, "When one takes a position of leadership, there is a very real danger of getting caught up in the hype surrounding that status ... Surround yourselves with people who will be honest with you about how you really are and what you are becoming, and then make them promise to not hold back... from telling you the truth."

Chapter 4: Sometimes Leaders Can't See What is Right in Front of Them

When you are at the top of the world, the most powerful nation on Earth, the most powerful nation in your region, the most successful company in your industry, the best player in your game, your very power and success might cover up the fact that you are already on the path of decline.

The question is how would you know?

In this book we will discuss the possibility of corporate decline, because some of the great companies we did look at in this book, Good to

Great and Built to Last, had subsequently lost their positions of prominence. On one level this fact didn't cause much anguish; just because a company falls doesn't invalidate what we can learn by studying that company when it was at its historical best.

But on another level we found ourselves becoming increasingly curious. How do the mighty fall? If some of the greatest companies in history can go from iconic to irrelevant, what might we learn by studying their demise, and how can others avoid their fate? Might it be possible to detect decline early and reverse course or even better, might we be able to practice preventive medicine?

We have come to see institutional decline like a disease; harder to detect but easier to cure in the early stages; easier to detect but harder to cure in the later stages. An institution can look strong on the outside but already be sick on the inside, dangerously on the brink of a precipitous fall.

Consider the rise and fall of one of the most storied companies in U.S. business history.

In the wake of the 1906 San Francisco earthquake, A.P. Giannini, founder of the fledgling Bank of Italy, found himself at odds with other bankers who wanted to impose up to a six-month moratorium on lending. His response; putting a plank across two barrels right in the middle of a busy pier and opening for business. "We are going to rebuild San Francisco," he proclaimed.

Giannini lent to the little guy when the little guy needed it most, and his bank, later renamed Bank of America (BAC), gained momentum; little guy by little guy, loan by loan, deposit by deposit, branch by branch, expanding ever outward from San Francisco. By 1945 it had surpassed Chase National Bank as the largest commercial bank in the world, and by the late 1970s it had grown to more than a thousand branches in more than a hundred countries. Along the way it became admired not just for its size but also for its quality of management.

Entering the 1980s, Bank of America held a revered position and was widely regarded as one of the greatest companies in the world. Within eight years it would post some of the biggest losses in U.S. banking history, rattle the financial markets to the point of briefly depressing the U.S. dollar, watch its cumulative stock performance fall more than 80% behind the general stock market, face a serious takeover threat from a rival California bank, cut its dividend for the first time in 53 years, sell off its corporate headquarters to help meet capital requirements, see the last Giannini family board member resign in outrage, oust its chief executive, bring a former CEO out of retirement to save the company, and endure a barrage of critical articles in the business press, with titles such as "The Incredible Shrinking Bank" and "Better Stewards (Corporate and Otherwise) Went Down on the Titanic." Anyone predicting such a fall as the decade began would have been viewed as a pessimistic outlier.

If a company as powerful and well-positioned as Bank of America in the late 1970s could fall so far, so hard, so quickly, then any company can. If companies such as Motorola (MOT), Circuit City (CCTYQ), and Fannie Mae (FNM) icons that once served as paragons of excellence can succumb to the forces of gravity, then no one is immune. If companies such as Zenith and A&P, once the unquestioned champions in their fields, can plummet from great to irrelevant, then we should be wary about our own success.

Every institution is vulnerable, no matter how great. There is no law of nature that the most powerful will inevitably remain at the top. Anyone can fall, and most eventually do. But all is not gloom. Leaders can substantially increase the odds of reversing decline before it is too late or even better; stave off decline in the first place. Decline can be avoided. The seeds of decline can be detected early and decline can be reversed (as we have seen with notable cases such as IBM (IBM) and Nucor (NUE)). The mighty can fall, but they can often rise again.

Chapter 5: Leadership Failures Sank the Unsinkable

The tragic fate of the Titanic over 100 years ago holds some important strategic lessons for CEOs who find themselves under pressure to achieve results fast. The street has no mercy nowadays. Results have to be delivered each and every quarter; year in and year out. Sometimes the fastest straight line from A to B is not in the best interest of a company's long-term survival.

The goal of the Titanic's captain was to get across the Atlantic as quickly as possible. As he reached the halfway point everything seemed to be going to plan.

Yet, unbeknown to all, the ship was heading for disaster as a direct result of his leadership. Not only were the crew and officers on board unaware of the captain's goal, but the singular pursuit of speed meant that the ship was hurtling along with few precautions.

There were no extra lookouts and little provision to react to the unexpected; when the iceberg was spotted the ship was moving too fast and could not be turned in time. One ship, the Californian, could have warned the Titanic and rescued survivors in the water. Yet the Californian, too, was lacking leadership and decisiveness. On this ship poor training, complacent assumptions and disorganisation were prevalent.

The need for speed

Much like the Titanic's captain, most executives of modern businesses would consider speed as a crucial element to their companies' success. Shareholders expect that from them. Unfortunately, like that captain, many leaders simply try to pick up the pace; often putting their faith in technology or process improvements and fail to pay attention to the people factor that is the key to true and sustainable speed.

The lack of strategic speed was clearly present on both the Titanic and Californian, just as it is in many of today's failing businesses. There are many analogies to be drawn between modern businesses and the disaster-courting ships as time gone by. Some businesses have strong leaders and a culture where the possibility of the unexpected is dismissed and not prepared for. Many of the banks caught in the subprime disaster are recent examples, as are the highly leveraged retailers who have become insolvent.

Others leaders are like the Californian, and fail to motivate staff sufficiently to ensure the organisation achieve its strategic goals. Ultimately, like that ship, they arrive too late. In contrast, the captain of the Carpathia changed course as soon as he knew there was trouble. The Carpathia was a cruise liner that was tasked with reaching the Titanic as soon as possible to rescue survivors.

The captain of this ship used speed strategically by clarifying the situation while in motion, posting extra lookouts and giving all crew members individual tasks and a sense of purpose. His actions meant their mission was executed flawlessly. Had these leadership qualities been in place aboard the Titanic, the catastrophe would most likely have been avoided in the first place.

Which captain are you?

The lack of strategic speed was clearly present on both the Titanic and Californian, just as it is in many of today's failing businesses. Had the captain of the Titanic focused on getting to New York safely (which is what his passengers and crew would have wanted) rather than on a pet goal of making fast time, the ship would have gone down in history simply as an opulent and fast cruise liner – a liner with a prosperous long-term future.

The question is whether your organisation is being led to achieve strategic speed, like the Carpathia, or moving too fast and recklessly, like the Titanic? Or perhaps it's bumbling along like the Californian?

The ability to achieve strategic speed; executing strategies and initiatives quickly is what separates successful companies from competitors who constantly have to play catch-up or fall by the wayside. The main quality that allows companies to move quickly is having leadership that creates clarity, unity and agility all across the organisation. One mutual goal and moving forward at high throttle.

A company that can achieve genuine strategic speed has a huge competitive advantage in these iceberg-ridden economic times. Those of us who study history or remember the movie may understand why. It wasn't the iceberg that caused the disaster. It is clear in our mind that the real cause was failed leadership.

Leadership is Responsible

Leadership is responsible for everything an organization does or fails to do. Leadership is more than a wooden figurehead. A leader is not a position, job title, or in this case, the captain of the ship. Leadership is not about power, ego or pride. Leadership is ever-present, touching, motivating, talking, checking and removing barriers, training, preparing, breathing and moving about. Leadership is not an entitlement; it is rather to be seen as a service, securing the organization moves ahead with a common sense of purpose and all women and men on deck.

The Titanic's ill-fated voyage was Captain E.J. Smith's retirement trip. He was headed for the easy life. All he had to do was get to New York in a record time. God only knows why he ignored the facts, why he disregarded seven iceberg warnings from his crew and other ships. The Titanic still rests on the bottom of the ocean, but we can resurrect the truth and apply a few lessons learned to help us become better leaders of today's businesses still afloat. To us there are 7 basic lessons to be learned.

1. The Biggest is Not Always the Best

Today's businesses must change course quickly. It took over 30 seconds before the Titanic turned away from the iceberg, but by then it was too late. The larger an organization becomes, the greater its inflexibility. The more difficult and cumbersome it is to steer, to direct and to change course. Large businesses soon grow into huge bureaucracies where rules, regulations, policies, procedures and "I need permission to make a decision" become predominant and the norm.

2. Rank Has Its Privileges

Ranking is good for command and control, but not good for change and innovation. Ranking people limits their potential. Today, businesses rank and classify people sometimes unintentionally. Whether it is reserved parking spaces for the privileged or being categorized as blue collar, white collar, temporary, part-time, those with cubicles or those with offices, the results are the same. Clear the lines between the classes and make everyone feel they are rowing in the same direction, for the same purpose. In a disaster, everyone is equal.

3. The Truth Constantly Changes

The Titanic was unsinkable, so they thought. The ship designers were so confident in their ship they only had enough lifeboats for half of the passengers. The thinking that made us successful yesterday will cause us to fail tomorrow. Our unlearning curve must be greater than our learning curve if we are going to succeed. Constant change is the norm in today's business world and leaders and organizations must be prepared to adapt rapidly to avoid dangerous "icebergs" ahead of them.

4. Technology Makes a Poor Substitute for Authentic Leadership

When technology fails, leadership must prevail. Years before the Titanic's voyage Captain Smith said, "I cannot imagine any condition which would cause the ship to founder. Modern shipbuilding has gone beyond that." Many businesses today have placed the wrong people in charge. They are not leaders, but managers. So when disaster strikes, who is going to step up and lead and keep the company securely afloat? Or will your technology cause you to shipwreck and pull you under?

5. Leadership is About Training, Development and Empowerment

As the stern of the Titanic lifted out of the water, the crew and passengers struggled with the lifeboats. There had been no drills, no rehearsals, and the crew stood unfamiliar with their responsibilities. The boats were improperly loaded and only one went back to try to recover survivors. A good leader helps people improve their skills so they can become more productive and he empowers them to make the right decisions on time.

6. What Lies Below is More Destructive than What is On Top

The greatest dangers lie unseen below the surface. That night in 1912 the water was smooth like glass and deceptively dangerous. The iceberg lurked below. Like steel fangs, it tore at the rivets along 300 feet of the Titanic's hull. Those below, the crew and steerage, felt and saw the damage first. Like a gasping breath, the steam billowed above as chaos reigned below. Then and now, those who know what is wrong with your "ship" are those below decks. Those people on the frontline usually have the best ideas and solutions to your problems. Consider empowering them and proactively ask them for their ideas and suggestions before catastrophe strikes.

7. Leadership Looks Beyond the Horizon

A good "Captain" is constantly on the lookout for shifting trends, submerged rocks, storms and icebergs. Wal-Mart founder Sam Walton identified and met a need while other retailers did not. Apple saw the need for the iPod while others were still happy with CD players. The vision of the Sony Walkman existed in Akio Morita's mind well before it entered the mind of the competition. Get the picture? Be on the lookout, scanning the horizon for the next wave of change instead of waiting for it to hit you in the face.

Chapter 6: Big Company Bureaucracy

When working with or within a large organization, it is important to keep it simple and stay focused on the goal so you don't get consumed by bureaucracy.

Even though many of us work in small teams or small companies, we also work with large organizations all the time. They are our customers, our suppliers, and our partners. Some of you may even have been successful enough to build your own start-up into a larger company that exhibits the organizational dynamics of a large corporation.

Even majority of SME (Small to Medium Enterprise) clients, investors and partners are from large organizations. In one instance, an SME that one of the authors used to work for acquired a company that was owned by a large bank, which was especially challenging given the bank's group decision-making culture and risk aversion.

We all understand the challenges of getting things done within a large organization. First, it is often easier for a large organization to say "no" than "yes". By saying no you are sure not to make any mistakes and expose yourself. Second, decisions often require involvement of multiple people, who all have busy schedules, and in some cases only a few people in a large organization make the majority of decisions. Finally, it's often hard to find someone motivated to make any change that involves risk for the individual and the company.

We recently sat down with one of our long-time friends who has successfully driven entrepreneurial-style decision making at a large company, first in various finance roles, then as CFO and CEO of a larger business unit. Based on this and our own experience as business practitioners there are four basic things that will help you to successfully navigate a larger organization.

1. **Do the Right Thing**

The first step is to explain how your idea, product or service will create the most value for the organization. In most organizations, saying "no" is a much easier answer than saying "yes". If you are pitching a product or service, build an offer-price combination that has clear and convincing benefits for the organization.

If the organization believes you are doing the right thing for them, you put up a barrier to saying no. Management then have to justify why they should NOT take action rather than why they should.

2. Build Supporting Relationships

In a larger organization, people need a reason to focus on something that they wouldn't otherwise, and most people will take a meeting with a person they like and trust. To sell your case, you need a motivated party to give you a fair hearing. A trusted relationship will take your meeting and can leverage their network within the organization to get you in touch with the right people to support your business proposal.

3. Don't Take No for an Answer

Even if you are doing the right thing for the organization, the first answer you receive will probably be no. It is just too hard for most organizations to push forward a change of any kind, even if adopting your new software will save lots of money.

When you get your first "no", set up a time to restate your position and ask them to explain why they said no. You may also want to have additional conversations with influential people in the organization to be sure that the "no" is warranted and not just a copout. Hence persistency is key to succeed with your proposal.

4. Punch Above Your Weight

In every conversation, show that you understand the needs of the CEO, shareholder, or any senior decision maker. You can demand the respect that you deserve when you show you can be a trusted partner for decision makers. If you are selling software and you aren't relevant to anyone but the software engineers, you will only get a meeting with the software engineers.

Getting things done within a large organization is more challenging, but it's critical to driving growth in most businesses. Focusing your efforts on the needs and dynamics of the organization will serve you well.

No one likes rules that make no sense. But, when top talent is complaining along these lines, it's usually a sign that they did not feel as if they had a say in these rules. They were simply told to follow along and get on with the program.

The great media companies were laying off employees recently by the truckload. They did not start with the feckless bureaucrats who were running the place.

The carnage in media jobs accelerated recently with hundreds getting whacked at Viacom, BBC World Service, NBC and Time Inc. One of the runners-up in the Person of the Year award by the industry website

IWantMedia.com was one of the Laid-Off Journalists. "We are in the middle of a volcanic realignment that is overdue; but as Big Media fights for its life; **are the right people leaving?**"

As great newspapers, magazines, TV networks, and publishing houses dismember themselves around us, it would be marginally consoling if the pink slips or P45 were going to those who contributed so vigorously to their companies' accelerating demise; the feckless zombies at the head of corporate bureaucracies who cared only about the next quarter's numbers, never troubled to understand the DNA of the companies they took over, and installed swarms of "Business Affairs" drones to oversee and torment the people under them. There are floors of these creatures in any behemoth media company, buzzing about each day thwarting new ideas or, worse, having "transformative" ideas of their own when what is usually required is to revive, with a bit of steadfast conviction, the originating creative purpose of the enterprise. It is the same with the auto companies.

The public rage towards the Big Three in the automotive industry reflects in part the rage many employees feel today about the way their own companies have been so messed up already that they were in no shape to survive a market collapse. Only now are we hearing how the innovative engineers who wanted to get into hybrids and electric cars were cut off when the accountants decreed that there was more and quicker profit in churning out gas guzzlers.

Same story with Moody's rating agency dissected in Sunday's New York Times by Gretchen Morgenson. Her interviews show how a company built on assessing risk for lenders became more concerned with serving itself. In the pursuit of ever higher profit margins (like 48 or 53 percent, for instance) it forsook its role as a watchdog to become a lapdog yapping for a bite of the master's sirloin.

What do cars, debt risk, and collapsing television networks have in common? The suits running them all lost sight of what they condescendingly call "product" i.e., whatever it was that motivated the company's spirit of excellence in the first place. The trouble is, those guys and their appointees didn't seem to be the ones leaving, did they? Indeed, the recent recession gave many of them air cover. "It's not my fault; it's the times we live in." "A lot of other Titanics are sinking, not only mine".

In many such big, lumbering companies every effort at innovation or practical efficiency gets strangled by something called "the established process". The cast of characters needed to reach a conclusion is eternally changing. One of the ironies of instant communication it seems is that no one is ever available to talk. Andy is at an offsite but he is on his BlackBerry. Maureen is at a sales meeting but she is at the same time on a conference call. What happened to Sir Alex? Oh, he's no longer officially around, but yeah, he is still "in the mix." You bet he is.

When a meeting finally convenes, there are still more people. Tramp, tramp, tramp in they come with their laptops, lengthy PowerPoint decks and their forecasts of why it is not going to work. Meanwhile, inside the company a "major restructuring" is announced and heads start to roll. The skills that took a lifetime to acquire are about to drain away. No one think that they really have the time to slog through the details of a project that might, incidentally, save this company.

Slowly but surely the talent drains away. It turns out that the two major best-selling authors only stayed at the mighty imprint because of that mousy middle-aged woman who really cared about their sentences. That is right, the one who just got laid off!

The talented TV director who made the network's last hit series got tired of talking to a voicemail and took his next successful show to the opposing network. The investigative journalist whose Pulitzers the chairman bragged about at awards ceremony dinners was told to crank out five half-cooked additional pieces a week for the website and guess what, the paper or network doesn't win prizes anymore and the public finds it increasingly irrelevant. At the once-great Knight Ridder Group of newspapers - The Miami Herald, Philadelphia Inquirer management was so harried to keep on raising already good profit margins it kept cutting the editorial operation until the papers went on the block. After the way the Tribune Company's CEO Sam Zell vengefully gutted the content of his papers is anyone surprised that we now learn the company whose assets include the flagship Chicago Tribune and once mighty Los Angeles Times filed for bankruptcy?

But perhaps in the turmoil the bones of original principles will emerge at last from under layers of dead skin and rotten management. Or perhaps the diaspora of talent will re-form and succeed while the companies who ejected them collapse and disappear.

Whether it is a high-profile tech company like Yahoo!, or a more established conglomerate like GE or Home Depot, large companies have a hard time keeping their best and brightest in house. Recent troubles at Yahoo! with a flat stock price, vested options for some of their best people, and the apparent free flow of VC dollars (venture capital) luring away some of their best people to do the start-up thing again.

Yet, Yahoo!, GE, Home Depot, and other large established companies have a tremendous advantage in retaining their top talent and we have seen the good and the bad things that large companies do in relation to talent management. Here is our Top Ten list of what we see large companies do to lose their top talent.

1. **Big Company Bureaucracy**

This is probably the number one reason we hear after the fact from disenchanted employees; however, it's usually a reason that masks the real reason. No one likes rules that make no sense. But, when top talent is complaining along these lines, it's usually a sign that they didn't feel as if they had a say in these rules. They were simply told to follow along and get on with the program. No voice in the process and really talented people say "cheque please."

2. **Failing to Find a Project for the Talent that Ignites Their Passion**

Big companies have many moving parts by definition. Therefore, they usually don't have people going around to their best and brightest asking them if they are enjoying their current projects or if they want to work on something new that they are really interested in which would help the company. Human Resources (HR) people are usually too busy keeping up with other administrative things to get into this. The bosses are also usually tapped out on time and this becomes a "nice to have" rather than "must have" conversation. However, unless you see it as a "must have," say adios to some of your best people. Top talent isn't driven by money and power, but by the opportunity to be part of something huge, that will change the world, develop themselves and for which they are really passionate. Big companies usually never spend the time to figure this out with those talented people.

3. **Poor Annual Performance Reviews**

You would be amazed at how many companies do not do a very effective job at annual performance reviews. Or, if they have them, they are rushed through, with a form quickly filled out and sent off to HR, and back to real work. Many such reviews are just "check the box exercises". The impression this leaves with the employee is that my boss and, therefore, the company isn't really interested in my long-term development and future here. If you are talented enough, why stay? This one leads into number four!

4. **No Concrete Discussion around Career Development.**

Here is a secret for most bosses; most employees don't know what they will be doing in 5 years. In our practical experience, about less than 5% of people could tell you if you asked however, everyone wants to have a discussion with you about their future. Most bosses never engage with their employees about where they want to go in their careers, not even with their top talents. This represents a huge opportunity for you and your organization if you do bring it up. A company one of the authors used to work for have separate annual discussions with their employees apart from their annual or bi-annual performance review meetings to discuss succession planning or career development. If your best people know that you think there is a path for them going forward, they will be more likely to hang around. Talent needs to know that there is a clear path forward. If they are a talent you should tell them so.

5. **Shifting Whims/Strategic Priorities**

We applaud companies trying to build an incubator or "brick house" around their talent, by giving them new exciting projects to work on. The challenge for most organizations is not setting up a strategic priority, like establishing an incubator, but sticking with it a year or two from now. Top talent hates to be "jerked around." If you commit to a project that they will be heading up, you have got to give them enough opportunity to deliver what they have promised before you put them on yet another project..

6. **Lack of Accountability and/or telling them how to do their Jobs.**

Although you can't "jerk around" top talent, it's a mistake to treat top talent leading a project as "untouchable". We are not saying that you need to get into anyone's business or telling them what to do; however, top talent demands accountability from others and doesn't mind being held accountable for their projects therefore, have regular touch points with your best people as they work through their projects. They will appreciate your insights/observations/suggestions as long as they don't spill over into preaching.

7. **Top Talent likes other Top Talent**

What are the rest of the people around your top talent like? Many organizations keep some people on the payroll that rationally shouldn't be there. You will get a litany of rationales explaining why when you ask. "It's too hard to find a replacement for him/her" "Now is not the time" however, doing exit interviews with the best people leaving big companies you often hear how they were turned off by some of their former "team mates". If you want to keep your best people, make sure they are surrounded by other great people.

8. **The Missing Vision Thing**

This might sound obvious, but is the future of your organization exciting? What strategy are you executing? What is the vision you want this talented person to fulfil? Did they have a say/input into this vision? If the answer is no, there is work to do and fast.

9. **Lack of Open-Mindedness**

The best people want to share their ideas and have them listened to however, a lot of companies have a vision/strategy which they are trying to execute against and often find opposing voices to this strategy as an annoyance and a sign that someone is not a "team player". If all the best people are leaving and disagreeing with the strategy, you are left with a bunch of "yes" people saying the same things to each other. You have got to be able to listen to others' points of view always incorporating the best parts of these new suggestions. Otherwise you may hit an "unexpected" iceberg in front of you.

10. **Who is the Boss?**

If a few people have recently quit at your company who report to the same boss, it is likely not a coincidence. It is an establish fact that most people don't leave companies, more often they leave because of their boss. One of the authors has several times been asked to come in and "fix" someone who is a great sales person, engineer, or is a founder, but who is driving everyone around them "nuts". We can try, but unfortunately, executive coaching usually only works 33% of the time in these cases. You are better off trying to find another spot for them in the organization or, at the very least, not overseeing your high-potential talent that you want to keep.

It is never a one-way street. Top talent has to assume some responsibility as much as the organization however, with the scarcity of talent which will only increase in the next 5 years; Smart Organizations are ones who get out in front of these ten things; that way you can at least try to avoid the most disastrous and '"Titanic icebergs" in front of you.

52

Chapter 7: Some Organizations' Culture is Like the Titanic

What is beneath the surface can sink the ship. An organization's culture is just a tip of the iceberg.

A strong culture provides consistency and attracts people who believe in the organization's mission and values. But, like the Titanic, the culture beneath the surface can sink the ship.

If you need help with culture alignment we would like to suggest that you can tell when culture and strategy are misaligned by looking at both leadership and employee symptoms. These two areas often reveal the need for culture alignment.

Leadership misalignment symptoms and quotes from business leaders we have talked to over the years:

1. "There is a great deal of distrust between employees from our legacy companies."
2. "We seem to be losing sight of our mission."
3. "We sometimes get lost in all the bureaucracy."
4. "Many of our strategies are focused on short term rather than long term solutions."

Likewise below employee misalignment symptoms and quotes from business managers we have dealt with.

1. "We have been experiencing high employee turnover."
2. "We need to be working more as teams than individuals."
3. "There are some adversarial subcultures at play in our company."
4. "Employee moral is lower than it has been in years."

Well-funded and well-planned culture change efforts have a history of failure. Why? Perhaps they are focusing on the wrong objective.

Organizational culture, or corporate culture, comprises the attitudes, experiences, beliefs and values of an organization. It has been defined as the specific collection of values and norms that are shared by people and groups in an organization and that control the way they interact with each other and with various stakeholders outside the organization. Organizational values are beliefs and ideas about what kinds of goals members of an organization should pursue and ideas about the appropriate kinds or standards of behaviour organizational members should use to achieve their goals. From organizational values develop organizational norms, guidelines or expectations that prescribe appropriate kinds of behaviour by employees in particular situations and they control the behaviour of organizational members towards one another.

For all we know, this definition is as good as any and there are many. Only the most optimistic individual can look at this conundrum of sociology and anthropology and not become overwhelmed. Secretly, many organizational-change consultants believe that corporate cultures cannot be changed. Anyone who has worked for a large company acknowledges that change of any kind is ponderously slow if the company changes at all. The analogy most often heard describing a corporation's resistance to change is that it is like "turning the Titanic."

Many leaders have tried various types of culture change initiatives. Well-funded and well-planned culture change efforts have a history of failure. A lot of time and money spent with negligible results, except the noticeable number of frustrated employees whose productivity has suffered from the time spent away from their jobs. Many employees feel they are trying to do things differently when the old ways are comfortable and seem to work perfectly.

An organization's culture is like a personality; personality and culture have similar characteristics. Both are complex; the relationship between various facets of their structure and function cause and effect, are difficult to isolate. You change one thing here, and it changes something else over there. The corporate personality has deeply rooted tendencies . . . traits . . . identifiable and predictable ways of responding that are akin to the things humans do that many consider to be genetically driven hardwired and, most of us have an intuitive feeling that most of these core "traits" are not changeable.

Many people would say, "It comes with the business". Some businesses, by the nature of the work and the types of people needed to do that work, have a unique identity much like a human personality. Trying to change the culture in a mining operation, an automobile plant, a chemical plant, a university, a dress manufacturer, or a software company to elicit "new ways of doing things - a new culture," is like trying to change a professional football player into a dress designer. There are "traits" that accompany these businesses that are not easy to change, and perhaps the idea of trying to do so is "fooling around" with something we should be attempting to understand, but not change.

It appears to us that most culture-change efforts fail because they do not discriminate between those facets of corporate personality that are hardwired (virtually unchangeable artefacts of specific businesses), and the more easily influenced behaviours associated with doing one's work. For instance, if you want an employee in a steel mill to work more safely, it may be easier to prompt him to remind a co-worker to "stand out of the line of fire," than it is to try a safety culture-change effort. In a typical culture-change initiative, the objective for the employee may be to "develop a commitment to safety," an objective which is laudable but abstract.

The ultimate objective of most organizational-change initiatives, culture change, or performance improvement initiatives is to change employee behaviour; what employees do (in very specific, micro-defined ways), how frequently they do it, when they do it, and the extra effort they exert (value-added behaviour). Interestingly, a unique quality of each culture is that much of the behaviour that is approved or disapproved is unwritten. Policies and procedures may demand one way of doing things, but practices the "way we do things around here," may require another.

Leaders have the ultimate influence on employee behaviour through the values they express in decisions, priorities, and promotions through all the consequences they apply to their direct reports which are then propagated through all the management hierarchies' companywide.

Most books on leadership and management attribute leadership style as the factor that most significantly affects employee behaviour. They imply that a leader's style translates into the values and priorities that control employee behaviour toward the customer and the product. Leadership style, values, visions, missions all form the background for employee performance, but more immediate, situational factors comprise the ultimate influence - the real "behaviour controls".

Leaders influence culture, but one would not fault any leader for throwing up his or her hands and allowing whatever consulting company to get hired to lead the organization down whatever special path they advise to evaluate, change or create the culture that is supposed to get the job done. Perhaps a leader's behaviour will change the organization's culture slowly, incrementally over time. More often, however, a leader's values and priorities quickly and directly influence employee behaviour, the behaviour of managers and supervisors toward their employees and hence the behaviour of the employees toward the work, the product, or the customer.

When reduced to its lowest common dominator, leader values and priorities translate into what an employee gets punished and rewarded for, the behaviour that his or her peers, their supervisor or their senior leaders sanction, applaud, allow, and approve. It is apparent that a change in leadership creates changes in an organization's climate, new priorities, performance expectations, and strategic direction and sometimes quickly. Parallel to these leadership-induced requirements, existing systems and processes the "old way of doing things," continues to exert influence on employee behaviour.

There is already too much literature and complex reasoning circulating about leaders, and their role in cultural transformation and managing change. We have a few simple suggestions that might simplify your understanding. We have heard them repeated by many subordinates of leaders repeated to us, but not to the leader himself or herself.

Leaderships' effectiveness in general, and in particular leaderships' ability to manage change would be enhanced if they were educated in the way employee behaviour is influenced by the culture, systems, processes, the physical environment, and supervisory verbal behaviour. Most leaders do not understand how immediate, real-time consequences influence what an employee does, how frequently they do it, or whether they stop doing it. Many leaders regard positive reinforcement, rewards, and recognition as necessary but not critical to business success. They often have a vague and incomplete understanding of what drives daily employee behaviour; this is a liability to the overall mission of the business and at best, a risk to profitability.

Changing a culture takes a long time. The straightest route to performance improvement and enhanced profitability is to change behaviour. Specifically identify the employee behaviour that will help the employee, work unit, or department excel and use behavioural strategies to increase the frequency and the strength of those behaviours. Use your knowledge of behavioural principles to control the factors that govern what an employee does on the job today, moment by moment. The management technology to influence behavioural probability is available. A supervisor can change an employee's job performance today! Immediately! But they can change it consistently for the better only if they really understand the given behaviour.

The key to employee performance and job satisfaction is the frequency and quality of his or her interactions with their supervisor. Work dialogs, what is said and how it is said to an employee, establishes the context for supervisors to say things that encourage or discourage the quality of an employee's work, the quality of the product, and their relationship with the customer. In a work dialog, the supervisor reinforces and punishes employee behaviour whether they know it or not. Leaders and all levels of management need to know how they impact employee behaviour and use that knowledge for securing positive influence.

Reward, recognition and incentive systems are often barriers to effective leadership. All levels of management can become dependent on programmed rewards as replacements for hands-on coaching and supervision. Existing reward systems directly encourage the behaviour that leads to the prize, the money, the payoff, or the award. A leader may be trying to create a customer-focused culture, while the existing reward systems may encourage cost control or productivity supported by behaviours that may make the customer a secondary factor or sometimes a nuisance. Reward and recognition systems should be evaluated for the impact they have on teamwork, quality, ethics and many other factors that can be usurped by compelling tangible rewards. Rewards and recognition practices represent an organizational system that influences other systems particularly the social system, human behaviour in profound ways. They often lull the organization into a sense of well-being - a quiet before the storm of unpredicted issues gather on the horizon - not noticing the iceberg in front of your Titanic.

If you want to change the way an organization functions, you better know what elements of the current culture to preserve and those parts to be changed. "The way companies do things" is a function of their business, their leadership and economic history, as well as the values and principles executed by current leadership.

Few leaders understand how their behaviour becomes a model for every level of management in the company, nor do they recognize that the things they reward and punish are incorporated into the things managers and supervisors also reward and punish. If a senior leader is defensive about or ignores new ideas, then every level of the organization does likewise.

If you understand behavioural principles, then you understand that each manager can choose the behaviours they will recognize or ignore. Most people who think about the benefits of culture change really want to change critical employee performance behaviours. Culture change is the wrong objective.

Chapter 8: Project Management Lessons from the Titanic Disaster

It is clear that the fascination with the Titanic has remained strong in the last century, so it may be worth considering what simple, yet often overlooked, lessons this famous disaster can still offer us, especially in terms of project management.

Based on our experiences as active business practitioners, we would like to offer you 12 simple pieces of advice:

1. **Learn to make adjustments**

Titanic's captain, Edward Smith, often receives the lion's share of blame for the disaster, and his obstinate belief that the ship could not sink helped lead to it being at the bottom of the Atlantic Ocean. When the ship's crew was warned about icebergs, did it move to Plan B? No, it carried on with plan A. When project managers spot trouble ahead, they have got to be flexible and get team members to chart a new course. They can't be so fixated on sticking to a timetable or a process that there are serious repercussions such as failing to meet the goal or doing so with great losses.

Our experience tells us that when working on a project, too many times the goals aren't clearly defined, and that often leads team members into rough seas that can soon have them floundering. When they need someone to pull them out, are there life rafts? Is the project set up from the beginning with safety measures to ensure that managers and stakeholders are on the same page? Or does lack of clear communication and organization endanger the project from the very beginning?

2. **Train the crew**

No one likes to contemplate failure, but the possibility is always there. Project managers can give team members the confidence to do their jobs by providing the right preparation and training. How many times have you heard heroic fire fighters or military service members say after a successful mission that it wasn't that big of a deal, because it was what they were trained to do? Titanic's crew had been so indoctrinated with the idea that the ship was infallible that they were unprepared when things started to go wrong. That led to a horrible outcome, and the same can be true for a team that isn't prepared by the project manager and given the right project management tools to do their jobs.

It's doubtful the fascination with the Titanic will wane any time soon, but project managers can still learn lessons over 100 years after it sank. They should take the lessons seriously to make sure their crews are trained for success but also for choppy waters ahead.

3. You need to know what you are measuring

Lack of lifeboats is a well-known matter, and it certainly played a role in the number of deaths; however did you know that Titanic actually did have enough lifeboats? According to the standards in effect at the time, the WEIGHT of a ship not the number of passengers determined the number of required lifeboats. Needless to say, these standards changed as a result of the inquiries into the disaster.

This principle applies to your own daily projects. Too often a project reaches the point of coding 90% complete, only to remain that way forever. Rather, we say, milestones should be objectively measurable. If you do not have valid measurements for your project, you too will run into problems. "90% complete business projects" can still have dangerous consequence and icebergs ahead.

4. Wrong assumptions can kill you

A few hours before the collision, wireless operator Jack Phillips received a message from a nearby ship, telling him of icebergs in the area; however Phillips at the time was taking care of messages to and from Titanic passengers and in doing so, was communicating with a lighthouse at Cape Race, Newfoundland. Unhappy with what he considered a bothersome message, and assuming it was unimportant, Phillips replied brusquely, "Shut up, I am working Cape Race!" As a result, Phillips never received the iceberg warning the ship was trying to send.

How often have we seen things blow up in our faces because of safe assumptions that later were proven to be wrong? Maybe we assumed that a particular system was using a newer software release than it actually was. Maybe we assumed that another department would take care of ordering cable. Maybe we assumed that the vendor received our critical email message. Assumptions are important in your work, but if you proceed on the basis of them, make sure everyone is clear about what assumptions you are making and test your original assumptions on an ongoing basis as the project "sails forward".

5. Distractions are dangerous

Of course, when we look back on an incident, we can always find fault with the actions of Titanic officers and crew. Still, because they certainly must have known about the risks of travelling through "Iceberg Alley," they should have focused the wireless operators less on passenger messages and more on communication with other ships. "Safety first".

The incident of the wireless operator, therefore, illustrates another hazard to project management; that of being distracted. How often do you start your work with the best intentions of completing your to-do-list, only to become side-tracked by chatting with co-workers or surfing the Web? If enough members of your team encounter enough distractions, your project will gradually fall behind.

6. Little things add up

A number of small factors played a role in the Titanic disaster. Allegedly, the lookouts had no binoculars, because those binoculars had been left behind at Southampton, where Titanic began her voyage. Jack Phillips interrupted a ship trying to send him an iceberg warning and neglected to deliver an earlier warning. While no one factor can be said to have "caused" the disaster, the effect of all of them made the disaster all the more likely.

How does a software project get to be a year late? One day at a time! If a major event or problem occurs, a project team rallies and steps up its effort however, such a team can fail to appreciate the issues of small delays and how those small delays (for example, illness of a team member or the postponement of a vendor meeting) add up. In other words, the small delays are just as critical as the large ones, meaning that adherence to milestones is critical to the success of any project.

7. Stakeholders should be kept informed

Following the iceberg collision, the nurse for the first class Allison family took one-year-old Trevor Allison from the family stateroom without saying where she was going. She and Trevor boarded a lifeboat and were rescued. However, because Trevor's parents didn't know about it, they spent the rest of the time looking for Trevor, turning down chances to escape in a lifeboat. As a result, the parents and their other child, three-year-old Loraine, died in the sinking.

Your own project might not be as critical as a sinking ship. Still, your stakeholders need to know about the status and progress of your project. Keeping them informed will keep them happier and it will prevent you from a lot of wasted efforts. In any important project time is money.

8. Other people's perspectives matter

One of the victims of Titanic was 23-year-old John Law Hume, a member of the band. A few weeks after the sinking, the company that managed the band sent a letter to his father, asking for payment for his son's band uniform. Even though such a request made financial sense from the company's perspective, it almost certainly sounded insensitive to Mr. Hume.

In the same way, when explaining aspects of a project, especially by technical members of your project team, try to see things from the other person's perspective. If a client asks a question, try to see beyond the question itself to the motivation behind the question. If a technical person is explaining a function of a system or program, make sure the explanation avoids jargon. Clear communication will lead to happier clients.

9. Moving targets can hurt you

The Titanic was one of three (at the time) new ships the White Star Line had built. The company's strategy was to emphasize luxury, not speed, as a selling point. Yet during that maiden Titanic voyage, White Star chairman J. Bruce Ismay reportedly pressured Captain Edward Smith to increase speed. This higher speed quite likely contributed to the collision, in preventing the ship and crew from reacting quickly enough.

In your projects, beware of "scope creep". Typical is the customer who says, "Can you make just this one small change please? The fact is any change is rarely small". Rather, it typically involves changes to other parts of a system, resulting in greater complexity, and requiring more testing. Make sure that your customer knows that in a project world governed by quality, time, and budget; at least one will have to yield. Be sure your customer understands the implications of a requested change and that the customer's expectations are appropriately set and managed.

10. Traceability is essential

A few days after the sinking, rescue ships based in Halifax, Nova Scotia, set out to recover victims and to return them to Halifax. As each victim was recovered, he or she was numbered accordingly. The recovery crew recorded information and a description of the victim in a ledger book and then bagged personal effects with that same victim number. If that victim was later buried in Halifax (150 victims were buried in three cemeteries there), that victim number was engraved by the grave marker. The victim number allowed researchers and others to link victim description to property description to cemetery location.

The same kind of traceability is important in your daily life projects. How familiar are you with the strategic objectives of your company? Can you find a logical connection between the requirements of your project and those strategic objectives? Of course, the connection might be a distant one, but there should be a connection nonetheless. But if you can find no such connection, you start asking yourself whether that requirement really is part of your system.

11. Methodology is more important than technology

When the recovery crews were recording victim information, they used regular ledger notebooks and pens obviously; no one had iPads, computers, or barcode scanners over 100 years ago. Nonetheless, the methodology they used had solid reasoning behind it, so it proved highly effective.

In the same way, you might want to use sophisticated planning and tracking software and tools. More important, though, is that your plan should be solid. The best software in the world will not save a poorly designed plan. Not over 100 years ago, not today or for the next 100 years.

12. Documentation may have lasting benefits

The documentation of the recovery records are still kept in Halifax, at the Public Archives. Researchers in Halifax and people from around the world still visit and review this documentation, over one hundred years after the fact. A few years ago, for example, researchers made use of these records as well as of DNA analysis to identify the "Unknown Child of the Titanic."

No one likes to document a project or system; however, documentation is often the most important part of a project because it may exist long after the project team has disbanded. That documentation might not need to exist for over one hundred years, but it should still serve the purpose of helping your customers understand their system. The documentation can also be helpful when designing similar systems in the future.

Chapter 9: Disaster Prevention Lessons Learned from the Titanic

The November 1999 Institute of Medicine report on medical errors captured the attention of the public and of lawmakers in USA. The report provided evidence that health care institutions can be pretty hazardous; from 44,000 to 98,000 deaths per year are related to medical errors, compared with about 42,000 deaths per year for automobile accidents, about 5,000 deaths per year in the workplace, and even fewer deaths per year for air travel.

The USA is not alone in focusing on medical error. In May 2000, Great Britain published an Organization with a Memory, a report from the chief medical officer on learning from adverse events in the National Health Service. In 1995, Australia published The Quality in Australian Health Care Study, pointing to the fact that there are far too many preventable errors that injure patients.

What do we call these medical errors? Terms such as "miss-adventure" and "adverse events" have been used, but we prefer "iatrogenic injury," which is defined as an injury causing harm to a patient resulting from medical management rather than from the patient's underlying or antecedent condition. It is important to separate an adverse event from the normal disease process, because a number of patients have antecedent conditions that may not be compatible with life. Death is a natural part of life. One of the reasons iatrogenic injury was not well recognized in the past was that death is not an unexpected outcome of medical care, whereas it is an unexpected outcome of car or air travel.

As we intensify our study of errors in medicine, we need to keep in mind that medical errors are not unique. They share many causal factors with errors in complex situations encountered with transportation, nuclear power, and the petrochemical industry. We can learn from those industries' efforts to study error and its prevention. In addition, we need to remember that errors can provide useful information and not just errors, but near misses as well.

Heinreich developed the iceberg model of accidents and errors. The part of the iceberg above the water represents errors that cause major harm; below the water are no-harm events or events that cause only minor injuries, as well as near misses. After studying automobile accidents for many years, Heinreich suggested that for every event that causes major injury, there are 29 that cause minor injury and 300 no-injury accidents

Sometimes the only thing separating an error that causes no injury from an error that causes major harm is pure luck or the robust nature of human physiology. A near miss is defined as an error process that is caught or interrupted; someone, usually an experienced staff member, intervenes to prevent the error. The goal in patient safety is to use the no-harm and the near-miss occasions to study their processes. Obviously, we have to respond to and learn from disasters, but if we want to be proactive, we need to deal with the less serious events that occur, which are much more numerous in our daily life.

In this chapter we will discuss the types of errors that can occur and apply the types to the Titanic disaster, errors that also occur in contemporary business life. We will then discuss how different organizational cultures respond to errors and consider the balance between discipline and voluntary reporting.

Types of Errors

Professor James Reason of Manchester University in England defined 2 types of errors; active and latent

Active errors are errors committed by those in direct contact with the human-system interface (in the case of health care, this are the healthcare professionals); they are often referred to as human errors. Individuals who commit these errors are those at the "sharp end." Their actions and decisions usually have an immediate effect.

Latent errors are the delayed consequences of technical and organizational actions and decisions such as reallocating resources, changing the scope of a position, or adjusting staffing. Individuals who commit these errors are at the "blunt end." Latent failures plus active failures lead to misadventures. Unlike the transportation industry, in which "the pilot is always the first to arrive on the accident scene," those who make the errors in medicine do not suffer the consequences of those errors. This creates an added responsibility and burden.

Jens Rasmussen, a Danish cognitive psychologist, further divided active error into 3 categories: skill-based behaviour, rule-based behaviour, and knowledge-based behaviour.

1. Routine tasks, such as driving a car, are examples of **skill-based behaviour**. We operate in a skill-based mode at work most of the time and do so superbly. The actions are so ingrained that we do them automatically, as if we were on autopilot.

2. Rule-based mode also involves familiar tasks but requires us to think for a moment and access stored information. An example of an error of **rule-based behaviour** would be applying the rules for a 4-way stop to a 2-way stop. We operate in this mode almost as frequently as we do in the skill-based mode.

3. We apply **knowledge-based behaviour** when we consciously solve a problem. Using the driving example again, most drivers would operate in a knowledge-based mode if they approached a broken stoplight. They may or may not remember to apply the 4-way-stop rule in this situation, and even if they did remember, they would know to do so cautiously, since predicting other drivers' responses is difficult. We rarely act in a knowledge-based mode unless we are in a new job or are learning something new. The capacity for error is highest in this mode. In fact, all change even just a change in a supplier can increase risk of error.

Our response to error is related to our organizational culture. An organization's culture is reflected by what it does in its practices, procedures, and processes rather than by what it claims to espouse or believe in. Ron Westrum has identified 3 types of **safety cultures**.

The first is **pathologic**; the organization says, "We don't make errors, and we don't tolerate people who do." This organization is likely to "shoot the messenger." Other organizations are **bureaucratic**; "If something occurs, we will write a new rule." At the other end of the continuum is the **learning or generative organization,** which seeks to understand the broader implications of error however, while organizations want to encourage information flow, they also recognize that some discipline may be associated with professional accountability. They have to do something about the employee who is truly dangerous while still encouraging reporting from conscientious employees.

Errors can be intentional, knowing, reckless, or negligent, and only the first 3 should elicit a punitive response. If the error was intentional, the person wanted to do harm. For example, he or she may have been mad at the organization and decided to destroy some equipment. This is rare. A person who knowingly made an error did not intend the error but knew that, by cutting corners, for example, the error might occur.

Behaviour such as working while intoxicated can be considered reckless whether or not an error occurred.

Reckless behaviour is not hard to identify, but it does not occur very often. The remainder of mistakes are examples of negligence. If we are negligent under the law, we are required to make restitution. Right now, our first tendency when our medical practitioners harm a patient is to keep quiet. We have to take more responsibility for admitting errors to our patients and working to fix those errors just as in automobile accidents, insurance information is exchanged and a settlement made.

The culpability of individuals on the Titanic

Using these guidelines, how culpable where those on the sharp end and those on the blunt end of the Titanic disaster? We need to recognize that knowledge of the outcome influences our objectivity, creating hindsight bias.

Whether Captain Smith knowingly or recklessly caused the error is questionable, but he was clearly negligent. He should have slowed down. He paid for that negligence with his life. Murdoch cannot be considered culpable, because he followed the standard procedure. Even Phillips, who was sending messages for the passengers, is probably not culpable.

What about the owner, Bruce Ismay? He certainly did not intend to cause harm, but it can be debated that he behaved knowingly or recklessly. At least, he was negligent. Andrews, the designer, was not culpable; all of these are our opinion at the time of writing this book however other evidence, event and history may proof us wrong. From the errors related to the Titanic disaster many parallels can be drawn to today's contemporary business life.

The higher in the organization one is the greater one's capacity to generate latent error. Thus, the lack of adequate lifeboats was the single greatest cause for the loss of life on the Titanic, and that was a decision made by the chief executive officer. Top management can sometimes be the enemy of safety. Everyone in the organization is accountable for his or her decisions and actions. If we hold people at the sharp end accountable for their actions and decisions, we have to hold people at the blunt end accountable.

The goal with patient safety is to reduce the risk of iatrogenic injury. We have to remove the hazards that increase the risk of injury. The British defines risk as the possibility or probability of occurrence or recurrence of an event multiplied by the severity of the event. Level 1 severity is death or severe harm; level 2, moderate or transient harm; and level 3, minimal or no harm.

The first step in error prevention and management is detection. Errors that are not detected can have disastrous consequences. A high reporting rate indicates a high detection sensitivity level (DSL), and a low reporting rate indicates a low DSL. To achieve a high DSL, an organization must eliminate impediments to reporting; confidential, no-fault reporting is usually the most successful approach. As the amount of information goes up, risk will eventually go down. Our national goal regardless the country you come from should not be to reduce medical errors but ultimately to reduce the risk of iatrogenic injury to patients. In doing so, we may find that there are actually more errors than we expected.

An organization that has a very high DSL can become overwhelmed. Many organizations see as much as 10-fold increase in reporting. There may be an initial "confessional stage," when employees bring up high-severity events from the past. If they become overwhelmed, managers should triage the investigation of events, highlighting events that represent the greatest risk either because of high occurrence rate or high degree of severity. Investigation involves gathering basic facts the who, what, where, when, and why; considering the number of barriers breached and the consequences; and recovering all pertinent documents. The investigators must get at the root causes and discover the latent errors. Otherwise, if they start with a human failure, they can stop there and fail to fix the system. As the management team investigates errors, the DSL rate may stay high; over time, however, the severity of events reported should go down.

In addition, the team should be able to identify process weak points, determine common causal factors, see where critical barriers to error are failing, and monitor the system for long-term changes. If errors continue to recur and the investigating team cannot identify a system error, it may be worthwhile to ask an outside group to do a process audit. Sometimes the individuals within a system are too close to it to recognize its problems. In populist language they can't see the forest for the trees.

A number of steps can be taken to effectively manage errors:

1. Identify system weak points before an adverse event happens.
2. Report near misses and no-harm events.
3. Encourage reporting.
4. Constantly look for root causes.
5. Avoid the blame-and-train trap.
6. Fix the latent errors that set people up for failure.

As we learned from the Titanic, latent errors make the greatest contribution to major disasters. We should never place too much faith in technological solutions without backup, and we should always expect the unexpected. By consciously trying to expect the unexpected the sinking of Titanic and many contemporary businesses could have been avoided.

Chapter 10: Image and Decision Making

When the RMS Titanic went to the bottom of the Atlantic Ocean in the early hours of April 15, 1912, it carried with it the era's uncritical faith in the promise of technology. The ship was the jewel of the industrial age. That such an extravagantly engineered behemoth could fall victim to the everyday risks of sailing the North Atlantic was more than shocking; it set off a period of deep scepticism about the relationship between man and his machines.

A series of inquests and reports laid out the reasons for the catastrophe and led to reforms in marine engineering and maritime law; but one risk factor couldn't be eliminated; human fallibility. We noted that the Titanic simply furnished another example of the well-established principle that if, in the conduct of any enterprise, an error of human judgment or faulty working of the human senses involves disaster, sooner or later the disaster comes.

In one respect, little has changed. As the recent loss of the Italian cruise ship Costa Concordia demonstrates, bad decision making can overcome even robust engineering. Virtually all man-made disasters including the Three Mile Island nuclear accident, the space shuttle Challenger explosion, and the BP oil spill can be traced to the same human failings that doomed Titanic. After 100 years, we must still remember and, too often, relearn the grim lessons of that night.

No disaster is a single event. Complex systems rarely fail without warning. Instead, accidents are the product of decisions made over hours, days, and sometimes years. Those choices are shaped both by the culture of the organization whether it is NASA or the White Star Line, which owned Titanic and by outside pressures.

On the morning of Jan. 28, 1986, the launch of the Challenger had already been postponed six times. Ever image conscious, NASA brass pushed to launch, despite the objections of engineers who worried that the rubber seals between segments of the vehicle's booster rockets might fail in the unusually cold temperatures. One of those engineers, Allan J. McDonald, recounts in his book "Truth, Lies and O-Rings" Inside the Space Shuttle Challenger Disaster that small quantities of combustion gases had leaked through the seals on previous missions. It was a warning sign but NASA came to accept the leaks as normal. Engineers were forced into the impossible position of trying to convince officials that their worries were valid. "Is it safe to fly is the correct question," McDonald tells Popular Mechanics, "not that you have to prove it will fail."

Like the space shuttle, Titanic was the technological pinnacle of its day. But a series of decisions from carrying too few lifeboats to using a rudder that may have been too small to enable the ship to turn quickly pared its margin of error. Those risks were compounded by unsafe operation. Accounts differ on whether White Star Line Managing Director J. Bruce Ismay urged Capt. Edward J. Smith to speed across the Atlantic in the hope of setting a record. But there is no question that the captain sailed the new and barely tested vessel through a region of known iceberg risk at nearly full speed on a moonless night. (A nearby ship, the SS Californian, had stopped for the night.) It was just one more bad decision along the Titanic's doomed path.

Success can breed complacency. During a career of more than four decades, the Titanic's Capt. Smith had been involved in only a single accident at sea, one that ended without loss of life. The New York Times noted that Smith's "rise in rank and importance was commensurate with the safe uneventfulness of his command."

Major disasters often occur after such long, uneventful stretches. Before the partial meltdown of the reactor at Three Mile Island in 1979, no U.S. nuclear plant had experienced a serious accident for 25 years. Similarly, before the blowout of the BP Macondo Prospect well in April 2010, the Deepwater Horizon rig had gone seven years without a serious mishap while drilling some of the deepest wells on the planet. "When you think you have a robust system, you tend to relax," Henry Petroski, a professor of civil engineering at Duke University, tells Popular Mechanics. Over time BP and its contractors began to cut corners; Alarms that would have warned of a gas leak were silenced, safety checks cancelled. The blowout preventer a last-ditch device intended to shut off a runaway well was only partly functional and workers were constantly urged to drill faster. That kind of culture invites trouble.

Technology can outpace judgment. The construction of Titanic came at the apex of a remarkable period of innovation in shipbuilding. Well before the launch of Titanic, Capt. Smith expressed supreme confidence in the state of maritime engineering: "I cannot imagine any condition which would cause a ship to founder," he said in 1907. "Modern shipbuilding has gone beyond that".

With three powerful engines, Titanic could maintain high speeds day or night. But the crew's ability to spot hazards was little changed from the days of sail. Two men stood in a crow's-nest scanning the horizon they didn't even have binoculars. The ship was equipped with the latest communications innovation, wireless telegraph, and in the hours before the collision the ship received five warnings about icebergs from other vessels. But at the time, the telegraph was seen primarily as a luxury service for passengers, and the crew had no firm protocol for acting on the information.

One message was handed to Ismay, who slipped it into his pocket, apparently unconcerned.

Similarly, at the time of the Gulf of Mexico blowout, BP and its contractors were pushing the art of undersea drilling into ever-deeper waters, using increasingly sophisticated equipment and yet the procedures to monitor and control these deep wells had not advanced much beyond those used in shallower seas.

Leaders may fail to plan for the worst. Just as Deepwater Horizon crews derived a false sense of confidence from their blowout preventer, the White Star Line put undue faith in the supposedly watertight compartments that composed Titanic's lower decks. The compartments were not sealed at the top; if the ship's bow dipped low enough, seawater would flow from one compartment to the next like water filling an ice cube tray. The probability of that happening? Low. The consequences when it did? Catastrophic.

So, the sinking of Costa Concordia feels sadly familiar. The ship was studded with technology what it lacked was good judgment by the people in charge. The captain approached too close to a rocky shore. Then, after the collision with an undersea outcrop, the crew rushed to reassure passengers that everything was fine. Had the crew quickly mustered everyone to the lifeboats instead, there might have been no loss of life. "A tool is only as good as the person that is using it," says John Konrad, a U.S. Coast Guard master mariner and author. "All the technology in the world can't replace a good captain." That remains as true today as it was over century ago.

What about your own company? Is everything going well? Are you starting to become complacent? Maybe it is time for you to carefully check if there are any icebergs in the horizon!

Chapter 11: Crisis Management Lessons from the Titanic

The 100th anniversary of the sinking of the Titanic few years ago caused many people to reflect on the glamour that was lost and the opportunities that faded.

It should now be clear to the reader that we think the Titanic can be used as a good analogy to business life. The Titanic was a monument to human folly and arrogance. It started with pomp and potential. But it turned into a lot of what-ifs and missed opportunities. So, too, is the case with business, which should learn the lessons from the recent economic downturn and corporate scandals.

On average, it costs six times the investment of preventive strategies to correct business problems (compounded per annum and exponentially increasing each year). In some industries, the figure is as high as 30 times...six is the mean average.

One of the greatest tragedies in history, the sinking of the Titanic, can be attributed to carelessness, insufficient planning, and stubborn pride.

People literally went down with the ship while still quoting the ship's marketing hype, "Everybody knows this ship cannot sink." They really believed the spin and rationalized it as a false hope to avert disaster. They were so sure, thought tragedy could not happen to them, believed themselves to be invincible, had false senses of security, and exhibited unnecessarily stoical behaviour when confronted with the harsh realities of death.

If any of following things had occurred, chances are that every life would have been saved. The Titanic would not have sunk if any of these precautions/actions had occurred:
1. **Management:** Had the ship's officers heeded one of the six iceberg warnings.
2. **Planning:** Had the ship's design required better lighting to see a potential collision or had the watertight bulkheads been one deck higher.
3. **Timing:** Had the ship hit the iceberg 15 seconds sooner or 13 seconds later.
4. **Supplies:** Had the ship carried enough lifeboats.
5. **Regulations:** Had the distress signal to a nearby ship been heeded and acted upon.

Not only did the people die, but it was the end of an era in travel. The credibility of steamships was shaken. Safety became more important in the luxury travel industry. Other forms of travel could serve customers better, faster, and cheaper. Concern about corporate savings at the expense of quality was raised.

Think of other disasters that brought similar concerns home and forced major changes in planning, policy, safety, implementation, and accountability:
1. Fires and collapses in commercial buildings due to use of substandard materials or improper safety precautions.
2. Citizen outcries over prejudice, hate, and bigotry actions by people in charge.
3. Unnecessary duplication of services by public sector and non-profit entities.
4. Chemical plant explosions.
5. Improper discharge of substances into the ozone.
6. Manoeuvres, where improper planning cost property and lives.
7. Insensitivity of organizations to their customers.

Most of us remembered when the blockbuster movie Titanic was re-released in 3D. With special glasses, audience/cinema-goers were able to see the ship crash into the iceberg even more vividly than before. In true Hollywood style, the film depicts a massive iceberg looming over the "unsinkable" ship with the crew scrambling to avoid a head-on collision.

We usually think of threats in this way; something big and dangerous that can sneak up and overwhelm us when we aren't looking. But the real story of the Titanic paints a different picture. It is a story that, while less dramatic, offers relevant lessons for leaders navigating their organizations through icy waters. Learning from previous disasters and being conscious of future dangers ahead can save both lives and businesses.

For business practitioners there are in our mind five key learnings:

1. You have Already Been Warned

The Titanic received six warnings of ice on the day of the collision. They were all ignored by the wireless operator, who was preoccupied with transmitting passenger messages and by the crew, who were more focused on breaking the speed record. So pay attention. Often the signs are already there if you listen and use your common sense. Some companies, like Borders, Kodak and Polaroid, ignored the signs and paid the price. Others, like Domino's Pizza, catched themselves before it was too late.

2. Size Doesn't Matter

The iceberg that the Titanic struck was not very big. It didn't even come up as high as the bridge of the ship and the hole in the boat was actually quite small; six cuts measuring a little over three square feet.

Our brains are wired to think of threats as coming from something bigger, but it is often the little things that become our downfall. Clay Christensen's work on disruptive innovation shows the power of David against Goliath, the mammal over the dinosaur, the start-up over the incumbent. Are you cognisant of any potential disruptive innovations within your own industry or have you become so successful and "unbeatable" that your vision is impaired by numerous blind spots?

3. It is What You Can't See

The iceberg that struck the Titanic was almost invisible. Continuous melting had given it a clear, mirror-like surface which reflected the water and dark night sky, like black ice on a wintry road. This type of iceberg is called a "blackberg." It is possible that the crew could have been looking right at the iceberg from a distance and not seen anything unusual. Are you on an ongoing basis actively looking for potential "blackbergs" within your own domain?

4. Look Below the Surface

Only about ten percent of an iceberg's mass is above water, with the other ninety percent below (hence the phrase "the tip of the iceberg.") With so much mass below the surface, it is almost impossible to push an iceberg out of the way. Even a ship the size of the Titanic couldn't push what looked like a small iceberg out of the way. Are you regularly looking "beyond the surface" of your current business successes? Sometimes listening carefully to your customers, taking an "outside-in" view on your business, may often reveal that there is a lot below the surface that your eye can not see directly.

5. Keep Moving

When First Officer Murdoch saw the iceberg, he put the engines in reverse and started turning away from the iceberg. It is a natural reaction to hit the brakes when you see a threat. But this action may have sealed the Titanic's fate. Ships turn more quickly when they have forward motion. If the captain had maintained the ship's speed or even accelerated, he might have avoided hitting the iceberg altogether.

So as you think about your business, think what warning signs you might have overlooked. Consider where the icebergs might be that you can't see, or where the threats might look deceptively small on the surface and when you do see a threat, beware of hitting the brakes; the best reaction might actually be to step on the gas.

"If something can go wrong, it will", says one of Murphy's laws. A crisis is a major occurrence with a potentially negative outcome affecting the organization, company, industry, publics, products, services or good name. A crisis interrupts normal business transactions and can sometimes threaten the existence of the organization.

With such a fully equipped ship and the best personnel, they didn't find it necessary to develop a crisis management plan (CMP) or a crisis communication plan (CCP). The ship couldn't sink, as they said, and nothing could possibly happen. There were medical facilities, for a worst case scenario and if help needed, personnel could radio other ships.

What would have happened if CMP had existed at the time?

A CMP would have detailed what would be done in the event of fire and other tragedies, how evacuation would take place, how to conduct practice drills for the crew and possibly passengers, who would lower the lifeboats, who would ensure that passengers were guided safely to the closest lifeboats and ships, who would contact persons ashore by radio when crew members would save themselves, and so on. A CMP would also include making sure effective insurance policies were in place.

The CMP would also include the crisis communication plan. This means it would include notification of the home office, where personnel acting as public relations professionals would in turn notify the press, White Star Line executives and employees and passenger's relatives. The CCP would also include the details about who would be the spokesperson. In Titanic case, Capt. Smith could have been the best person if he had survived, but Smith went down with the ship; however the Managing Director of White Star, J. Bruce Ismay, was on board, survived and was rescued from a lifeboat sent from the Carpathia.

As media communications, there were two persons involved from White Star. Harold Bride, a radio operator on the Titanic who worked for Marconi Wireless Telegraph Company, one of the survivors picked up by Carpathia. He wrote the first account of the tragedy that he sent to the New York Times by wire from the rescue ship. Phillip A.S. Franklin, who had been hired to head White Star's New York office, called together a kind of crisis communication team.

Headlines after the tragedy

The morning before the sinking, New York Times ran a story announcing that the "The New Giantess Titanic" would soon arrive in New York, as part of a PR campaign of brand-awareness.

Other newspapers' headline indicated that the editors were much less aware of accurate details of the story. Many newspapers assumed that the passengers were rescued, if not everyone, the majority. After the first press conference, the journalists were so amazed of the official news that the Titanic sank, that they all left to call the news and not hear the rest of the details.

Does your own company have a CMP/CCP in place? Or will you play it "by the ear" should an iceberg show up in your horizon?

Beyond the tragedy and the impressive amount of lives lost in the accident, after 100 years, the Titanic still remains an interesting subject to discuss, from many points of view and there are relevant lessons to be learned for contemporary business life.

Chapter 12: Crisis Leadership/Business Continuity Lessons

Many "What Ifs" could have and should have been asked even before the voyage of Titanic began. What if the Titanic had enough lifeboats for everyone? What if Captain Smith had heeded the warnings of ice and altered the course or slowed down? What if, what if, what if....

Are there any crisis leadership/business continuity lessons to be learned from the tragedy that apply in today's business environment? Absolutely! In our mind, based on literature studies, our own practical experiences and common sense there are 10 basic lessons to be learned:

1. **Understand and read the environment:** Slower speed could have prevented the Titanic accident. In treacherous terrain, it is important for all of us to have high situational awareness and to the very best of our ability, be aware of what is going on. Situation awareness involves being aware of what is happening in the vicinity, to understand how information, events, and one's own actions will impact goals and objectives, both immediately and in the near future. This is critical in managing a crisis.

2. **Humility is still a great virtue:** The ship's officers were overconfident about their ship and their abilities. Humility is a great virtue and one that will serve you well, in all situations...crisis or not. Assume that something actually could go wrong.

3. **Lead:** It is important that those in the position of leadership do just that, lead! A key aspect of that leadership is the willingness to make a decision and then execute on that decision. There was much hedging going on in the early stages of the Titanic emergency and leadership was in short supply. Leadership is easy to assume during success and "tail winds". Real leaders will show their true value during tough "head winds" and crisis situations.

4. **Communicate, Communicate, Communicate:** Poor communication seems to always be one of the top learnings in any disaster. It is essential to have a well thought out external and internal communication strategy. The external communication was challenged by the Marconi wireless telegraphy system on board the Titanic. It was innovative and probably too cutting-edge to be effective. Not many people knew yet how to operate and receive Marconi messages. The internal communication was poor especially to the third class passengers. No formal ship wide announcement was made that Titanic was sinking. People who heard murmurs of an emergency dismissed them. At large proper and timely communication will often make a difference on how you successfully navigate out of difficult situation faced on day-to-day business life.

5. **Have a plan at hand:** Remember the Titanic was unsinkable and when you actually believe you are unsinkable, why have a plan?! There was no plan because it wasn't supposed to happen. We must have plans, they must be usable, executable and current even if you believe nothing will ever happen to your company. A disaster recovery plan at hand is the foundation for getting well out of any significant crisis situation.

6. **Activate early on:** The evacuation order was given too late. By the time people realized it

was "bad", it was too late. Passengers were reluctant to board the lifeboats and most of the lifeboats placed in the water were less than half full. Companies are no different. They keep thinking it will get better. The IT department is known for saying, "Give me 15 more minutes, I know we can fix it!" There is nothing wrong with activating and then stopping if you resolve the issue. In other words it always better to be safe than sorry.

7. **Training is essential:** The Titanic crew was not familiar with the procedures to evacuate the ship and launch the lifeboats. The time to learn your procedures is not when you need them but well in advance. Training is critical and pays off when emergencies occur. The same goes for contemporary business life. If people know exactly what to do in a crisis situation the better off you will be. Who is doing what, when and why?

8. **Exercises are a lifesaver:** The crew's inability to respond quickly and appropriately wasted time and cost lives. We fall back to our level of training and humans learn best by doing. We need to do regular exercises to ensure an appropriate response.

9. **Have the appropriate equipment:** The Titanic didn't have enough lifeboats; there were 1,178 lifeboat seats and 2,200 people. The regulation was based on the ships tonnage, not the number of passengers. Do

you have the equipment that you need to respond and recover in a disaster situation? Does your staff know how to use the supplies and are they up-to-date and prepared and capable of using the available tools in an emergency situation?

10. **Conduct a post-mortem investigation:** Once an incident is over, stop and evaluate what you did right and wrong and plan a course of action to correct current deficiencies. The follow-up to the Titanic disaster resulted in major changes to maritime law that impacts us all even today. Learn from your failures and plan a course of action to correct them. Do you really learn from your mistakes in business life? Mistakes in business life are inevitable. They are okay as long as you and the organization learn from them in order to avoid similar mistakes in the future.

What the Titanic did then and continues to do today, is to remind us that the practically unsinkable is indeed sinkable and too big to fail is indeed fail-able and that the unthinkable could and often can happen. Key to effective crisis management is thinking through what could actually happen. Don't get nervous or paralyzed by doing so; however, having carefully thought through what could actually happen makes you much better mentally prepared when the crisis suddenly shows it's ugly face. The lesson; learn from history as it is likely to repeat itself. With that wisdom in mind you are much better prepared to steer your own "company/ship" through "icy waters".

Chapter 13: Business Contingency Planning

A well thought out business contingency plan can mean the difference between your business survival and failure if business disaster strikes. A fire, a flood, a hard drive failure or data theft; any or all of these could put your business out of commission. Taking the time to do some business contingency planning will help ensure that your business is able to resume operations in the shortest possible time.

Using common sense we suggest that you use the following 11 steps to create a basic business contingency plan:

1. **Determine what the main risks are to your business.**

Is it data theft? Flooding? Earthquake? Figuring out what types of business disasters are most likely will help you focus your business contingency plan and not waste time and money preparing for something that is very unlikely to happen. There is no point in planning how to recover from an earthquake, for instance, if your business is not located in an earthquake zone. Order your risks by likelihood of happening and impact should they happen. Pay most attention to the high probability/high impact ones.

2. **Prepare an evacuation plan.**

Go over it with personnel and post it conspicuously throughout your business premises. How will personnel know they need to evacuate? What should they do when they are notified of an evacuation? What routes are available out of the building(s)? Where should personnel meet outside of the building(s)? Who is responsible for checking to see that everyone is out safely? Do regular exercises with staff to proof your plan is working in real life.

3. **Create a communications fan-out system.**

If something happened at your business, who would be responsible for notifying each person who works there? Ensure phone and email contact lists are up to date and that the people responsible for contacting others have printed lists as all technology fails sooner or later and usually at the most inconvenient time.

Also decide who will be responsible for communicating with the public and how (press releases, signs in the windows, radio and television announcements etc.)

4. **Be sure that your on-site emergency kits are complete and up-to-date.**

This Emergency First Aid Kit Checklist for Businesses shows exactly what first aid kits for businesses need to contain. Depending on what types of business disasters may happen in your area, you may want to add other supplies. For example, one gallon of water per person per day is one of the recommended supplies on this list of Emergency Supplies for the Retail Store.

5. **Take steps now to protect your business data.**

Your business data is one of your most valuable assets. If it was stolen or destroyed, would your business be able to quickly get up and running again or even carry on at all? 6 Rules of Data Protection explains how you can get the peace of mind of knowing your business data is protected and will be accessible again quickly.

6. **Ensure your business carries adequate insurance.**

Fire insurance is the type that springs to mind, but fire is certainly not the only possible business disaster your small business could experience. Besides other obvious physical disasters such as flooding or wind damage, consider the damage that could result from theft, for instance and then there is the potential liability factor if your small business is engaged in activities that might open you up to lawsuits.

Choosing the proper type of insurance to cover your risks and having good, up-to-date insurance coverage will go a long ways toward getting your small business up and running again if disaster strikes.

7. Decide what would be absolutely essential for your business to start operating again if a business disaster closed you down and take steps to ensure that those essentials would be available quickly.

One of the business owners we interviewed on contingency planning said "In the case of our primary business, IT development, we basically need our business data and a computer or two and we could be back up and running". Your business may need more people and materials before it can reopen. Which people are key to your operations? Do you need particular equipment? Perhaps an arrangement can be made with another business that has the equipment you need. Would you need certain supplies? Find out now who the alternate suppliers or shippers would be.

8. Get to know your neighbours.

Opening the lines of communication with the business owners around you can really benefit your business contingency planning. Let them know what you are hoping to do and see if you can get them involved. You might be able to share the costs of some expenses related to contingency planning or make tit-for-tat arrangements to help each other out in case of disaster.

9. Check out local programs and resources.

Your city or town may have contingency plans, disaster response plans in place or provide resources that will make it easier for you to put your own business disaster plan together. See what is available in your town before you start writing your own business disaster plan.

10. Put it all together.

As you work through your business contingency plan, put all the pieces together in print form. (Digital copies are nice but not very useful if the power goes out and/or digital devices can't be used.) A three-ring binder works well. Include your business's evacuation plan, communication plan, information about emergency kits and insurance policies, data protection measures and operational essentials, as well as details of any arrangements you have made to keep or get things up and running again.

11. Keep your business contingency plan handy.

Last but not least, you want to make sure you keep your business disaster plan in an easily accessible place and make sure everyone who needs to know where it is knows its location. You should also assign one person and a second to grab the business contingency plan on the way out if the business disaster necessitates leaving the premises.

It is easy to put off business contingency planning. There are always immediate "crises" that demand our attention. But how significant are they really compared to an event that shuts your business down for hours, days or weeks? Taking the time to prepare a business contingency plan will have a huge payoff if business disaster ever strikes.

The above advice may seem more suitable for small to medium size enterprises; however our experience tells us that even many bigger multinationals are worse off when it comes to proper contingency planning. Following the 11 basic steps is a good starting point whether you are "big" or "small".

Chapter 14: Managing Multicultural Teams

If you work in a multicultural team, you are fully aware of the benefits of bringing people together with different backgrounds, ideas and cultures into a team. When managed well, a team of different viewpoints can be a real strength for an organisation. Diversity offers dynamism, energy and creativity; however, if managed badly, a multicultural team could turn into a sinking ship.

Managing a multicultural team requires foresight, planning and above all a humble recognition that things can go wrong. Was the Titanic not known as "the unsinkable ship"? Arrogance in a team's infallibility is not healthy, ever. Good managers need to actively look after their teams to ensure smooth communication and that all members are on the same page and working for a common purpose. A good manager is always thinking about potential dangers and potential responses; not resting on laurels and assuming "everything will be okay".

Icebergs

It is big, white, cold and if you hit it, you will sink. What is it? Yes the iceberg! Funny enough, when trainers talk about culture in courses about cultural awareness they often use the iceberg as a metaphor for culture. Why? Because, like culture, you never really see the whole thing; you only ever really see the tip above the surface which can lead to people underestimating the damage the iceberg (culture) can do. Ignoring the impact of culture is like ignoring the iceberg. Not advisable.

Unconscious biases

As managers we carry a lot of unconscious biases in our luggage. The subject has been extensively studied by Cook Ross over the past 2 decades. They describe how this bias stems from our natural inclination to distinguish "friend" from "foe" in order to survive. Our background and personal experiences create the prism through which we see, interpret, and judge the world. In other words we see the world as we are ourselves, not as it necessarily is. Our decision making and talent management systems can therefore be seriously infected with bias. A good starting point is therefore to recognize and accept that you have such biases; only by doing so you can start to make much more objective decisions when selecting the right members for your team.

Staying on course

If you find your team is headed towards an iceberg, you should learn from history that changing course isn't always the best policy. Titanic steered to try and avoid hitting the iceberg whereas experts say if it had stayed on course, there would have been less damage. A good manager of a multicultural team should not avoid conflict or confrontation. Within a multicultural team this is common as cultures clash, however a good manager helps the team stay on course and use differences within the team to the team's advantage by helping them find ways of complementary solutions and common ground by nurturing their creativity. Our experience tells us that a team full of diverse players often produces much better innovative and sustainable results than a bundle of likeminded individuals.

Clear communication

Clear and effective communication is key within any team and especially so when the members interpret the world in different ways. When you think back to the Titanic, part of the reason for the tragedy was that there was initially a hope of rescue; however the flares that were fired were misinterpreted as celebratory signals as opposed to signals of distress. The message here is simple; miscommunication can lead to the sinking of the ship and it is up to the manager to make sure all team members communicate and interpret messages in the same way despite their different and diverse cultural backgrounds.

Sink or Sail?

So, what could have saved the Titanic and what can managers of multicultural teams take away from this analogy? Simple – you need to be proactive and alive to the dynamics of your team. Waiting to see what happens isn't good enough. Managers need innovation and foresight. Managers need to be culturally aware. How have you built your team? What "culture" do they share? How can team members complement each other? How do they communicate and work with one another? What happens in emergency situations? Do you have enough lifeboats for everyone? Do you know how to operate the lifeboats should an emergency occur?

A recent example was when a major international software developer needed to produce a new product quickly, the project manager assembled a team of employees from India and the United States. From the start the team members could not agree on a delivery date for the product. The Americans thought the work could be done in two to three weeks; the Indians predicted it would take two to three months. As time went on, the Indian team members proved reluctant to report setbacks in the production process, which the American team members would find out about only when work was due to be passed to them.

Such conflicts, of course, may affect any team, but in this case they arose from cultural differences.

As tensions mounted, conflict over delivery dates and feedback became personal, disrupting team members' communication about even mundane issues. The project manager decided he had to intervene with the result that both the American and the Indian team members came to rely on him for direction regarding minute operational details that the team should have been able to handle itself. The manager became so bogged down by quotidian issues that the project careened hopelessly off even the most pessimistic schedule and the team never learned to work together effectively.

Multicultural teams often generate frustrating management dilemmas. Cultural differences can create substantial obstacles to effective teamwork but these may be subtle and difficult to recognize until significant damage has already been done. As in the case above, which the manager involved told us about, managers may create more problems than they resolve by intervening. The challenge in managing multicultural teams effectively is to recognize underlying cultural causes of conflict, and to intervene in ways that both get the team back on track and empower its members to deal with future challenges themselves.

During our personal careers we talked to numerous managers and members of multicultural teams from all over the world. These discussions, combined with our deep knowledge on dispute resolution and teamwork, led us to conclude that the wrong kind of managerial intervention may sideline valuable members who should be participating or, worse, create resistance, resulting in poor team performance. We are not talking here about respecting differing national standards for doing business, such as accounting practices. We are referring to day-to-day working problems among team members that can keep multicultural teams from realizing the very gains they were set up to harvest, such as knowledge of different product markets, culturally sensitive customer service, and 24-hour work rotations.

The good news is that cultural challenges are manageable if managers and team members choose the right strategy and avoid imposing single-culture-based approaches on multicultural situations.

The Challenges

People tend to assume that challenges on multicultural teams arise from differing styles of communication but this is only one of the four categories that, according to our personal experiences, can create barriers to a team's ultimate success. These categories are direct versus indirect communication; trouble with accents and fluency; differing attitudes toward hierarchy and authority; and conflicting norms for decision making.

Direct versus indirect communication.

Communication in Western cultures is typically direct and explicit. The meaning is on the surface, and a listener doesn't have to know much about the context or the speaker to interpret it. This is not true in many other cultures, where meaning is embedded in the way the message is presented. For example, Western negotiators get crucial information about the other party's preferences and priorities by asking direct questions, such as "Do you prefer option A or option B?" In cultures that use indirect communication, negotiators may have to infer preferences and priorities from changes or the lack of them in the other party's settlement proposal. In cross-cultural negotiations, the non-westerner can understand the direct communications of the Westerner, but the Westerner has difficulty understanding the indirect communications of the non-westerner.

An American manager who was leading a project to build an interface for a U.S. and Japanese customer-data system explained the problems her team was having this way. "In Japan, they want to talk and discuss. Then we take a break and they talk within the organization. They want to make sure that there is harmony in the rest of the organization. One of the hardest lessons for me was when I thought they were saying yes but they just meant 'I'm listening to you."

The differences between direct and indirect communication can cause serious damage to relationships when team projects run into problems. When the American manager quoted above discovered that several flaws in the system would significantly disrupt company operations, she pointed this out in an e-mail to her American boss and the Japanese team members. Her boss appreciated the direct warnings; her Japanese colleagues were embarrassed, because she had violated their norms for uncovering and discussing problems. Their reaction was to provide her with less access to the people and information she needed to monitor progress. They would probably have responded better if she had pointed out the problems indirectly for example, by asking them what would happen if a certain part of the system was not functioning properly, even though she knew full well that it was malfunctioning and also what the implications were.

Chapter 15: Lessons from Lehman Brothers

What do the Titanic and Lehman Brothers have in common?

Both went down on a Monday, the worst day of the week for workers and the stock exchange alike.

Monday is the only day the stock market is more likely to fall than to rise and the two worst days in market history are both known as Black Monday. There is no single reason why Mondays are so blue. Then again, there is no single reason the market rises or falls on any given day, driven as it is by the whims of traders placing millions of individual buy and sell orders.

Some anecdotal evidence comes to mind; companies are prone to release bad news on Friday nights, when fewer people are paying attention. Monday is the first day investors can react and when companies collapse, they often do it late Sunday or early Monday, after spending a last weekend trying to stay afloat. See Wachovia, Bear Stearns and, most famously, Lehman Brothers investment bank, on September 15, 2008.

Lehman was headed directly for the biggest subprime iceberg ever seen, but unlike the captain of the RMS Titanic, CEO Dick Fuld and his No. 2, Joe Gregory, didn't try to swerve. There were plenty of warnings. In June 2005, Michael Gelband, Lehman's new global head of fixed income at the time, declared the U.S. real estate market was pumped up like an athlete on steroids. With amazing prescience, Gelband said that Countrywide, New Century Financial, and other aggressive lenders had created $1 trillion in economic activity that was built on "false money" and was sure to falter. Other executives made similar warnings about excessive leverage.

Fuld and the others in Lehman's "ivory tower" ignored the red flags. When the company's risk expert, Madelyn Antoncic, became bearish in 2006, the myopic CEO started excluding her from meetings on big deals. Then he fired her.

Others, like Gelband, quit, dismayed their insight was ignored. Fuld didn't bother to retreat when the U.S. mortgage market started to unravel in 2007. Instead, he disastrously decided to diversify by scooping up hedge funds and commercial real estate and by making private equity deals and the company relied on borrowed money to do so. In mid-2008 a group of top executives led a coup that dethroned Gregory and seemingly stripped Fuld of power. The new president restocked the management team, even bringing back Gelband. They tried to save Lehman, "fighting for the bank they all loved" but it was too late. On Sept. 15 2008, Lehman sank.

Over 5 years after Lehman Brothers, could another big bank fail?

A week before it happened, it was unthinkable. Afterwards it was seen as inevitable, just the first domino of the great 2008 financial crisis. Now, over 5 years after Lehman Brothers ceased to exist, we see if anything has been done that would stop such a devastating failure happening again.

From its humble origins as a general store founded in 1844, Lehman Brothers rose to become America's fourth-largest investment bank. Lehman became renowned as a tough, scrappy competitor, winning business against global giants such as Goldman Sachs, Morgan Stanley and Merrill Lynch.

Under aggressive chief executive Dick Fuld, Lehman's stock soared as it rode the US housing boom. At its peak in February 2007, this storied bank was worth $60 billion and had 28,000 employees.

But when the US housing boom ended in mid-2006, prices of mortgage-related securities began to fall. Lehman had huge exposure to poor-quality "subprime" mortgages and other assets with free-falling prices. In August 2007, things got worse when a global credit crunch froze inter-bank lending markets.

In March 2008, Wall Street colossus JPMorgan Chase bailed out Bear Stearns, buying the beleaguered bank for a fire-sale price of $10 a share after Bear experienced liquidity problems. When Lehman's credit ratings came under threat six months later as it struggle with cash outflows, no white knight rode to its rescue. On 15 September 2008, Lehman Brothers filed for bankruptcy with liabilities of $613 billion and assets of $639 billion. Over 5 years on, this remains the largest corporate insolvency in history.

Lehman's legacy

The sudden collapse of this Wall Street giant sent shockwaves around the world, with the UK stock market crashing by more than a fifth (21%) in a single week. As stock markets plunged other banks trembled on the brink, the US Treasury rescued AIG, eventually pumping more than $182 billion into the global insurer. Merrill Lynch was saved by falling into the hands of Bank of America, sold for $29 a share in a $50 billion takeover. Eventually, a total of 15 US banks went bust in 2008, mostly regional and smaller lenders.

As the global financial crisis worsened in October 2008, the UK Government used huge sums to prop up banks. Billions in bailouts, billions more in lending guarantees, forced mergers and when banks wouldn't merge they were partly nationalised with the rest handed on to anyone who would take them. Bradford & Bingley was carved up between Santander and the treasury, HBOS pushed into Lloyds TSB's arms while money was flung at Royal Bank of Scotland (RBS). Interest rates were slashed from 5% to 0.5% in less than six months.

How Lehman wiped out wealth

Before Lehman fell, fears over dodgy subprime mortgage securities and credit default swaps meant little to the typical Briton, with many shrugging off these seismic dislocations in world markets.

But that didn't protect them; Lehman's collapse ignited a firestorm that destroyed many trillions of pounds/dollars of wealth. The typical "man on the street" suffered a devastating fall in his personal wealth, thanks to the plunging values of homes, shares, pension funds, insurance policies and other investments.

By the lows in March 2009, world stock markets had roughly halved from their peaks, erasing vast sums from portfolios. Even worse, in property-obsessed Britain (with £4 trillion of our total personal wealth of £7 trillion invested in bricks and mortar), house prices began to tumble. From their peak in mid-2007 to the lows of spring 2009, UK house prices fell by an average of around a fifth (20%).

With asset prices tumbling and debts rising, everyone in Britain from richest to poorest lost out as the bubbles bust. Charles Bean, deputy governor of the Bank of England, warned during the depths of the disaster: "This is a once-in-a-lifetime crisis, and possibly the largest financial crisis of its kind in human history."

Lehman's legacy lives on today just like the Titanic legacy.

Over half a decade after Lehman Brothers bombed, the effects of the global financial crash are still keenly felt in the UK.

British taxpayers are nursing losses of tens of billions of pounds on total liquidity support of £1.5 trillion advanced to banks. This is a sum equal to the United Kingdom's entire economy (known as gross domestic product or GDP). Speaking of GDP, following the longest and deepest recession in living memory, the UK's output is still 3% below its 2008 peak. This is an unprecedented economic slump in British history.

A smaller economy means less money, the UK unemployment rate has swelled from 5.8% in August 2008 to 7.8% in August 2013 up more than a third (34%) in five years.

The cost of living has also climbed steeply since Lehman fell, with wage rises lagging behind inflation. Today, real (inflation-adjusted) incomes are at a 10-year low. In contrast, with the Bank of England's base rate stuck at an all-time low of 0.5% since March 2009, ultra-low mortgage rates (such as two-year fixed rates below 2%) have eased the strain on mortgage borrowers.

With savings rates plunging, British savers have never had it so bad. With most accounts offering before-tax rates below 2% a year, savers have missed out on vast sums in interest as rates plumb new depths.

UK house prices have yet to reach their previous peaks, except in parts of the South East and, notably, London, where prices have surged to new highs on foreign demand for homes in the capital. While the falling pound has made UK assets cheaper for foreign buyers, overseas holidays have become more expensive.

Furthermore, with public spending soaring and tax revenues diving, UK national debt has more than doubled. Today, it exceeds £1.2 trillion; it was just £525 billion in March 2008 at the end of the 2007/08 financial year. Even after rounds of spending cuts and tax rises by Chancellor George Osborne, the Treasury continues to spend £10 billion a month more than it collects in taxes. That means an extra £400 of debt per month for each of the UK's 26 million households.

In the aftermath of the financial crisis, governments and regulators across the world enacted new legislation to make banking safer, aiming to avoid more TBTF (Too Big To Fail) bailouts. In the US, UK and Europe in particular, financial watchdogs and law makers have brought in curbs on the riskiness of banks.

In the UK and Europe, regulators aim to reduce risk in banking by improving two key measures of banks health. First, new rules have pushed up the level of free capital basically their emergency savings - banks hold, known as their "Core Tier One capital". As a result, many UK banks now have around 10% of their total assets in free capital a sharp contrast to the 0% (zero) free capital Royal Bank of Scotland (RBS) at its taxpayer bailout.

Second, regulators aim to lower banks leverage ratios (which show a bank's equity capital divided by its total assets). In the UK, the Prudential Regulatory Authority (PRA) wants all major UK lenders to have a leverage ratio of at most 3% by summer 2014. Thus, no UK banks should have total assets exceeding 33 times its equity – Lehman's approximate leverage when it failed.

Will it work?

Despite regulatory tightening, future banking crises remain on the cards. Rising house prices, looser credit and a return to growth will help banks forget (or disregard) the lessons of Lehman. Even risky credit derivatives are sneaking back into the market.

House prices are already starting to rise steadily in the UK, fuelled by Government support from the "Help to Buy Schemes", plus cheap loans from the Bank of England's Funding for Lending Scheme. Already, commentators have warned of another potential bubble being blown in house prices.

The UK has already experienced a banking emergency this summer, when the Co-op revealed a £1.5 billion shortfall in its balance sheet. This black hole emerged after uncovering huge losses in commercial mortgages and business loans on the books at Britannia Building Society, Co-op's ill-fated buy in 2009. As a result, Co-op bondholders face losses, while savers are protected by the £85,000 safety-net provided by the Financial Services Compensation Scheme.

In short, another Lehman is a distinct possibility; especially if a country were to exit the euro, causing a firestorm in European markets. With continental banks yet to fully write down their impaired property loans (especially in Spain), another round of big write-offs is still a reality.

To trigger another banking crisis, all it takes is a toxic trio of hidden losses (for example, in commercial real-estate loans), falling asset prices and market volatility. As we saw the sinking of Titanic catastrophe repeating itself with a modern Concordia version, we cannot ignore these possibilities, so we must dare to imagine more Lehman-like let-downs in the medium term.

Chapter 16: Three Traps That Make the Glory Days Fleeting

There are a few, but many of the world's top companies in 1985 have foundered, shrunk, grown obsolete, or been acquired by rivals that grew stronger. General Motors and Ford, the world's two biggest carmakers in 1985, spent the last decade in a dizzying tailspin, bleeding cash, losing market share, and struggling to turn themselves around. Venerable industrial firms like ITT restructured and drifted down the Fortune 500, while Wal-Mart, Verizon, banks, and technology firms displaced them. Digital Equipment and Wang Laboratories, once leading computer firms, disappeared completely. Even resurgent titans like Apple and IBM stared into the abyss of irrelevance and made painful changes before clawing their way back to the top.

Most companies, of course, never get to the top, and the few that do find it daunting to stay there. Vijay Govindarajan, a professor at Dartmouth's Tuck School of Business and co-author of The Other Side of Innovation, says "successful companies tend to fall into three traps that make the glory days fleeting". First is the **physical trap,** in which big investments in old systems or equipment prevent the pursuit of fresher, more relevant investments. There is a **psychological trap**, in which company leaders fixate on what made them successful and fail to notice when something new is displacing it. Then there is the **strategic trap**, when a company focuses purely on the marketplace of today and fails to anticipate the future. Some unlucky companies manage a trifecta and fall into all three traps and sink like the Titanic.

With today's rapid technological change, companies rise and fall faster than ever before. The list below represents 10 companies that were once the most innovative in their industry and then lost their edge. It is no Hall of Shame; most of these firms remain able competitors that might innovate their way back to greatness one day. Rather, their stories illustrate the way missed opportunities and tunnel vision can send even a mighty enterprise off-course. The lessons apply to many firms, whether large or small. Here are 10 firms that enjoyed enviable success, followed by unenviable stumbles.

1. **Blockbuster**

This video-rental chain survived the transition from VHS to DVD just fine; but then failed to adapt to the next big change. Blockbuster remained flat-footed when Netflix started sending videos through the mail, cable and phone companies started offering video-on-demand, and Redbox started renting videos for a $1 a night through vending machines. Now that video streams through computers and phones, Blockbuster's conventional retail outlets seem hopelessly outdated. The firm is closing hundreds of stores, working off debt, and copying some of its competitors' moves, with a fighting chance to catch up. But it's now chasing its industry instead of leading it.

2. Dell

Back when IBM and Hewlett-Packard still sold most of their products through stores, Dell had a different idea. Cut out the middleman and sell directly to consumers. When the Internet arrived, Dell took off and competitors got whiplash trying to keep up with its skyrocketing sales. But a decade later, Dell faltered as mobile devices began to displace PCs, cheap Asian machines cut into profitability, and big customers began to demand end-to-end service, not just hardware. Dell has countered with mini-laptops, smart phones, and other trendy products, but it's now following the pack.

3. Eastman Kodak

For nearly a century, no company commercialized the camera as successfully as Kodak, whose breakthroughs included the Brownie camera in 1900, Kodachrome colour film, the handheld movie camera, and the easy-load Instamatic camera. But Kodak's storied run began to end with the advent of digital photography and all the printers, software, file sharing, and third-party apps that Kodak has mostly missed out on. Since the late 1980s, Kodak has tried to expand into pharmaceuticals, memory chips, healthcare imaging, document management, and many other fields, but the magic has never returned.

4. Microsoft

It helped give the PC mass-market appeal, and still dominates much of the software industry. But Microsoft has also fumbled or passed up many great ideas that others capitalized on, like Web TV, E-books, smart phones, and the tablet PC. Why didn't they commercialize any of this? The problem is execution. Sticking to one business line can be risky, especially in an industry as fast changing as technology and sure enough, the market is shifting away from the PCs that Microsoft's software is designed for.

5. Motorola

Its first big success came with car radios, which led to two-way radios, which eventually led Motorola to build and sell the world's first mobile phone. Motorola dominated that business as recently as 2003, when it introduced the trendy Razr, the biggest-selling mobile phone ever at the time. But Motorola failed to focus on smart phones that can handle e-mail and other data, and rapidly lost share to newcomers like Apple, HTC, and Samsung. Motorola was vanquished so swiftly that its cell phone division became a perennial money-loser and the firm has to spin it off into a separate company, allowing the core Motorola to focus on networking equipment and a few other areas.

6. Sears

Many people still call it the Sears Tower, but Chicago's tallest building is now officially the Willis Tower, named after a British insurance broker that is one of its main tenants. Sears moved out long ago and also surrendered the spirit associated with such an architectural landmark.

In earlier days, Sears put catalogues on the map, sold suburban Americans many of their household belongings, and introduced sturdy, affordable brands like Craftsman and Kenmore. But later in life, Sears stood flat-footed as competitors like Wal-Mart, Target, and Amazon chewed up its turf. Sears has dabbled in insurance, financial services, real estate, Internet service, and many other business lines as it has tried to find its way. Yet it's still looking for a winning strategy, and is now paired with Kmart in a kind of faded-glory holding company. Analysts think a Web strategy might ultimately save the firm as stores continue to vanish.

7. Sony

Not long ago, the Walkman was as ubiquitous as the iPod is today, and Sony dominated the market for TVs, cameras, video recorders, and many other consumer electronics. But as Sony became a huge conglomerate with film and music divisions, it lost leadership in many of its core product lines. What tripped up Sony and some of its competitors was the move from hardware to software, which put the emphasis on the brains of the device rather than the circuitry. As a result, faster-moving competitors like HTC, Samsung, Vizio, Apple, and the various makers of cell phones which of course come with cameras these days have outpaced this old-school innovator.

8. Sun Microsystems

Lucky timing only lasts so long. This computer start-up began building high-end servers just as the computer revolution was revving up, and it foresaw the virtues of networking and universal software that could run on any computer. Its Java programming language, introduced in the mid-90s, became an industry standard just as the Internet arrived, helping make Sun an industry giant by the late 1990s. But the dot-com bust wiped out many of its customers and changed the way companies meet their technology needs. As PCs became more powerful, fewer big customers needed Sun's costly servers, and Sun spent most of the last decade downsizing and retrenching. With Sun's market value just a fraction of what it had once been, Oracle bought the company.

9. Toys "R" Us

This retailer thrived in the '80s and '90s, as its concept for specialty megastores aligned with a surge in American consumption. As it went national, Toys "R"

Us drove many competitors out of business and gobbled up others. Then the tables turned, with the once-mighty toy giant suddenly bested by discounters like Wal-Mart and Target, online sites like Amazon, and smaller merchants with better quality and service. Toys "R" Us has been in turnaround mode since 2004, when private investors bought the company. The rehab has involved store closings, layoffs, and downsizing, with the owners hoping a public offering will help raise cash to pay down debt taken on back when the firm was rapidly expanding.

10. Yahoo

When Web search and aggregation were still virgin territory, the pioneering Yahoo tried to charge for services like e-mail and file sharing, while upstart Google offered everything for free. Customers flocked to Google, which surged to a commanding lead in search that it still holds. Yahoo still grew into a huge Web portal, with strong sports, financial, and news coverage that generates billions in advertising revenue, but it also drifted into job-hunting services, video streaming, original entertainment, and other ventures it has since sold or folded. Yahoo's snub of a $45 billion buyout offer from Microsoft in 2008 now looks like a huge gaffe, since Yahoo's market value has fallen since then.

Have you looked for the 3 traps within your own company? Are you actually on board your own Titanic heading full throttle towards the icebergs? Are you still making big investments in old systems, equipment or obsolete products at the end of their life cycle? Is your company obsessed with what made you successful so you can't see the disruptive icebergs in the horizon? Finally ask yourself if you are so entailed with today's marketplace; that you are unable to anticipate the future? Watch out for the icebergs. Be sure they are there somewhere in the horizon.

Chapter 17: Accountability

Lack of accountability is sort of like the Titanic; you know it's going to sink, but when?

It's not my personal responsibility!

One of the most sacred tenets of management is the need for clear accountability. At the outset accountability sounds straightforward. In simple terms it is about the acknowledgement and assumption of responsibility for actions, products, decisions, policies etc. As such, organizations spend enormous amounts of time and energy defining jobs, roles, and goals and then figure out who to reward or punish when things go well or poorly. The assumption of course is that people will perform more effectively if they know exactly what they are supposed to accomplish and what will happen if they make or miss the target. The word also implies that "accountability" cannot exist without proper "accounting practices." To put it differently; absence of accounting means an absence of accountability.

The reality of organizational life is never quite so black and white. More often than not, accountability is muddled, rewards are misapplied, consequences are watered down or never occur, and people do not see the direct connection between results and recognition. As the senior manager of a large technology firm said to one of us; "If you work hard and get good results here, you will be rewarded; and if you don't work hard and get mediocre results, you will also be rewarded.". Also the press has covered numerous cases of companies with catastrophic Titanic-like-results where senior management still cashes out mega bonuses.

From our experience, there are three common reasons why organizations fall into accountability traps like these.

1. **The first is the complexity of your organization's structure.**

Most companies have some version of a matrix, with a combination of enabling "functions" (such as IT, HR, and Finance) and line business units. In many cases there are further distinctions between "head office" and "field" units, and multiple levels of geography-based teams (regions, districts, countries). Trying to nail down accountability across these structures is extremely difficult, especially when each one has its own budget and priorities.

In a large healthcare company, for example, the person technically accountable for a major customer has to work with the leaders and staff of at least six other organizational units, many more senior than her, in order to get anything done. This makes it virtually impossible to hold either the customer-leader, or any of the other unit heads, accountable for results.

2. **Compounding the complexity of the organization structure is the fact that work processes are constantly evolving, and cut across different units.**

Because of these upstream and downstream interactions, it's often difficult for people to know whether their actions have impact, or how changes in one part of the workflow will impact others. As a result, it's easy for managers and employees to say that they did their jobs well, and any problems must have been caused somewhere else.

3. **The third and most significant reason for fuzzy accountability is that people work hard to avoid it.**

There is truth in the old saying, "Success has many parents, but failure is an orphan." Managers are quick to take credit for good results, but are often reluctant to accept responsibility for failure. This is especially true in cultures that blindly punish people for missing their numbers, trying things that don't work, or delaying deadlines in the face of other pressures. To avoid career-limiting consequences, managers go through all sorts of gyrations to diffuse or re-direct accountability, such as; blaming others, referring to circumstances outside their control, shifting resources to other areas, reorganizing, changing measurements mid-stream, or any number of other creative deflections. As a project manager once told one of the authors, "We can use one snowstorm for many months as an excuse for being late with our deliverables."

So yes, accountability is difficult to nail down. But it's not impossible. Start out by doing the following 3 basic things:

1. First, try to understand the reasons for unclear accountability. Use the reasons above as a starting point for a discussion with your team and your managers. Identify the cultural patterns that characterize your organization and think about ways to overcome them.

2. Second, make it clear who is accountable for what and how results will be measured. Make sure you set these rules before starting any cross-functional assignment. At the same time, communicate the upside of success and the downside of failure, so no one needs to guess what will happen.

3. Third, appoint process champions. Especially for activities that cut across different parts of the company, process champions will have end-to-end responsibility for achieving the desired metrics. These are difficult roles to play since they often come without full authority for all of the resources, but they are a step in the direction of single accountability for dispersed activities.

Passion within the workplace

Does the topic get your attention? It should, but not because this chapter addresses romantic relationships at the office or the romance at the famous Titanic movie. We are talking about company leaders creating passion as in a boundless, extremely fervent fondness and commitment for the job and company. In fact, in every organization, one of the major roles of the leader is be a passion maker, or someone who is responsible for developing and inspiring enthusiasm within the entire chain of command.

One of the most powerful ways successful leaders create passion is by setting up an effective system of accountability, which is measuring performance and taking appropriate action. Understanding the crucial role of accountability in the workplace, and using it to drive a business' success and impassion its workers, is more than possible and that is the best-kept secret when it comes to top-of-the-line leadership. A true leader also "walks the talk" and assumes responsibility for his or her personal actions.

Simpler said than done, a lack of accountability is one of the biggest reasons why companies struggle and sometimes fail. Oftentimes, it's not managed consistently and fairly because leaders focus on the negative and people mistakenly associate it with only discipline and punishment. In today's business environment, many CEOs and managers are feeling the pain related to this lack of accountability, and, consequently, company "sins" are surfacing. These business leaders need to take immediate corrective action to create strategic alignment to their vital goals and drive performance through a strong accountability system.

A Closer Look at the Accountable at Workplace

One way to understand accountability is to examine a workplace that doesn't have any. What does it look like? When there is a lack of accountability, a company tends to resemble what is called a "country club" culture, as opposed to a "jail-like" culture. The "A players" often end up leaving because they crave and deserve accountability, and get frustrated when good performers are not recognized and poor performers are not held accountable. Conversely, such businesses struggle to attract top talent because those types of employees want to be in an environment that values accountability.

In addition, the company without accountability does not perform to its potential, and standards are allowed to slip low. Things just don't get done, and because the organization is not performing as is expected, moral suffers, too. People who should not be there drag the company culture down, complacency and mediocrity are accepted. As a result, more and more of the responsibilities weigh on the shoulders of the company leader, the superhero who carries the full burden of the organization and is often overwhelmed because he or she hasn't pushed accountability down into the lower tiers of responsibility. A vicious downward spiral is in progress.

On the other hand, a company with thriving accountability looks quite different. Accountability enables a leader to create ownership for the company on behalf of its employees. That means developing ownership for problems, successes, goals, initiatives, people and results (getting things done). Accountability sets the controls in place, drives the business, and indicates what is and what isn't on track. Through accountability, leaders always make three important discoveries.
1) Whether they are on the right course.
2) Whether they have got the right people in the right places.
3) Whether their people are achieving their goals.

With these findings, leaders gain insight on instituting change and setting new objectives.

How Passion Plays Into the Accountability Picture

Accountability holds leaders to the task of clearly defining goals for the company and its people, as well as establishing measurements to assess those goals and define success. It is this accountability that provides an opportunity to assign ownership to company and personal performance objectives, measure results and follow through with regular objective evaluations.

When people own a piece in the goal-setting puzzle and achieve what they set out to do, this is highly rewarding and motivating for each individual involved. Even more so when the leader follows through with positive recognition, acknowledging the team players for their achievement. The result of this is that people become impassioned about their role in the company's welfare and their own professional development is something that is actually quite personal and close to the heart. This new found passion is the driver for productivity. It incites people to work harder, dream bigger and excel beyond their wildest imaginations. In this case a positive upward spiral has been generated. It is self-perpetuating.

Accountability can be a highly positive experience for a leader, the team players and the company at large, which is contrary to the notion that accountability connotes something "negative". Often associated with the term "feedback" and viewed as derogatory if results have not been accomplished, accountability can provide opportunities to coach someone, counsel that person and enable growth. It also provides leaders with the chance to develop their own skills, such as learning how to have difficult conversations about poor performance.

Accountability provides the chance for all to improve upon their weaknesses and position and propel a business toward a place of prosperity. It's this uplifting, highly positive and evolutionary experience that creates passion in the workplace. It's simply become an invigorating place to be.

Roadblocks to Accountability

Accountability can be a possibility for your company, only if several common roadblocks are avoided. First, whether you are a company owner, manager or team leader, set aside the natural tendency to confuse accountability with not being liked. In your position, avoid crossing the line of getting too close to people. Instead, focus on earning the respect not friendship of professional peers. Remember, when it comes to infusing passion into the workplace, your job is to create loyalty to the company, not loyalty to you as a person. Persons come and go but healthy company exists for centuries.

Second, you will be seriously challenged if you fail to set goals and expectations on a continual basis. Equally important is making sure people understand the goals and expectations, and what is required of them. Everyone involved needs good goal criteria; for example, not just measuring the number of activities, but the results and of course the goals should be realistic but stretching.

Third and lastly, you can't get complacent because customers are not complacent, the market isn't complacent, investors aren't complacent, and so forth. Strong leaders recognize that when success results are achieved, the bar must be raised. When it's not, passion will wane, and productivity will be at-risk. Sure, this will be a challenge, but if a company doesn't grow, it sinks like the Titanic. Your ultimate job is to build and sustain a thriving organization and one thing is for sure; creating passion through accountability is arguably one of the most important, best-kept secrets you must know to achieve such a track-record of success.

Almost all organizations talk about the importance of accountability, but making it happen isn't so easy. What is your experience? Start by accepting accountability yourself.

Chapter 18: Lessons for Modern Business Leaders

It doesn't take a business school professor to see the parallel with the Titanic catastrophe during recent years; whether it is banks becoming overloaded with high-risk sub-prime loans, or businesses achieving growth and profits by leveraging themselves with huge debts that are only payable on the most optimistic of all assumptions.

It is easy to see these analogies with the wisdom of hindsight, yet in 2006 many of the people and organisations that are now pariahs were being lauded by shareholders, employees, politicians and the media for their great achievements.

The crew of the SS Californian has even more analogies for modern business leaders. Its badly led crew failed to correctly warn the Titanic of the icebergs, misinterpreted the signal rockets, missed the distress calls, and misread the limited information they received.

The Californian arrived on the scene too late to make any difference; belatedly realising the Titanic had sunk. Poor training, miscommunication, and inaction were on display all stemming from the attitude of its captain and officers. When the time came for it to make the big difference in this world it failed lamentably.

How come that many organisations, despite the rigours imposed through the recession, fall into this category?

These stand in stark contrast to Captain Rostron of the SS Carpathia, the ship which arrived on the scene as quickly as it could and rescued the survivors in the lifeboats (but sadly too late for those in the water).

When it first started to receive worrying information, rather than ignoring ambiguous messages or making complacent assumptions, the Carpathia's captain changed course, and clarified the situation while in motion. Extra lookouts were posted to reflect the speed and all crew members were prepared with tasks and sense of purpose ahead of the rescue, which was executed flawlessly.

It exhibited good leadership, and clear purpose, executed by a well-trained crew. If the Carpathia had been as near to the Titanic as the Californian, the outcome would have been so much different.

The financial crisis has given us lots of iconic corporate Titanics in recent years from the banking sector. The ensuing recession has also sunk lots of corporate Californians, but many have plodded on too, and still survive keeping their heads above water.

The leadership lessons from the Titanic apply to businesses today as much as they did to the ships at this iconic event.

The question is whether you are the CEO on a corporate Titanic, Californian or Carpathia. If you are on the Carpathia then great, how can you keep excellence going? More likely you are on a Titanic or Californian whose leaders think it is well run and unsinkable. CEOs need to reflect carefully on their organisation, and what they can be doing to make sure their business has the leadership it needs to ensure survival in these continuing iceberg-ridden economic times.

We dedicated our book to the corporate sailors that keep their ships afloat. Keeping their companies healthy and afloat was and still is the name of the game for the leaders in today's contemporary and ever changing business world.

Chapter 19: Managing People on a Sinking Ship

As the continued bad news from Blackberry reminds us, no company's future is secure. When your business is facing declining sales, a potential buy-out, or even certain closure, how do you manage people who are likely panicking about their future? How do you make sure they don't abandon your sinking ship? Can you keep your team's motivation and productivity up? The short answer is yes. Even when it's clear that a company is in trouble, there are ways to help team members stay focused, deliver results, and weather the storm.

Instead of abandoning best common practices, the most skilled leaders reinforce them. Good management is good management. Treating people well, helping them flourish, and unlocking potential are all good practices regardless of the environmental circumstances.

Okay it is not easy to keep people enthused, engaged, and working hard when they know the company may not be around but it is not impossible either. Here are six principles we suggest you follow when your organization starts to feel like a sinking ship.

1. Look for opportunities to turn things around

Sometimes it is clear that the end is near. Your manufacturing plant is slated to close. A larger company has bought your business unit; but in other situations, there may be a glimmer of hope. There is often a short window of opportunity to do something differently. If there is a chance of saving the company, focus your team on doing two things. First, seek input from customer-facing employees. Their front-line perspective could provide valuable insight into how your company needs to change. Second, do small pilot experiments with alternative business models. You ask what kinds of products and services would customers welcome that we don't offer today? The goal is to alter the organization's course away from the one that got you into this mess.

2. Give your team a larger purpose

To keep people focused, give them something to work toward. Identify a profound purpose that is more important than the individual benefit. People want to believe their work matters in any situation. This can be tough when the company's success is no longer the goal but you might select something that employees value personally leaving a legacy. For example the manager leading a GM plant that was going to close in two years inspired the employees who knew the end of their time with GM was near, he told them to do their very best so that senior leaders would be sorry when closing day came.

3. Provide reasonable incentives

Find ways to reward good work. After all, if the company is failing and employees are going to collect a pay cheque anyway, why wouldn't they spend their last three months on Facebook? It is the leader's job to answer the question. What is in it for me? Make clear what they will get if they do their best in this trying time. Will they learn a skill that will help them find their next job? Will the acquiring company be keeping some staff? How will the experience help them grow professionally? If you can't find a way to truthfully explain why they should help you get the job done, you are out of luck.

4. Show people they matter as individuals

Don't just offer the same things to everyone, however. People want to still be seen as individuals.

Tailor your message and the incentives to specific team members. Whenever possible, give them personal attention and care. When news of the crisis hits, meet with your employees one-on-one. We suggest you say something like; we want you to flourish and will do our best to take care of you even though we may not be here in the future. Find out what matters most to them and do your best to meet those needs. There may be some people who can't handle the uncertainty; in those cases, do what you can to help them find a position at another company.

5. Be honest and authentic always

We are adamant that being transparent is crucial in these circumstances. Whatever you know, share it with your employees, be as honest as you possibly can. Don't try to protect people from the truth or ignore what is happening. You can't not talk about reality and don't say anything you don't mean. In tough situations like these, people are on high alert for lies and inauthentic messages.

6. Don't ignore emotions

People are going to be upset, afraid, and angry. Don't pretend that these feelings don't exist. Instead, make room for them. You don't want to dismiss emotions. It only drives them underground and makes them more deeply felt. It is important to acknowledge feelings, especially negative ones. Tell people that you are available to talk whenever they want. Encourage people to get together without you so that they can say things they might not want to express in front of a boss. The best practices we have seen are lots of huddles people getting together and just having conversations about what is going on. Don't play the role of psychologist though. If people need more specialized support to deal with what is going on, refer them to outside help, such as trained outplacement counsellors.

In summary:

Do:
    a. Focus people on a meaningful goal.
    b. Be 100% honest about what you know; share any information you can.
    c. Encourage your team to get together without you to talk about what's happening.

Don't:
    a. Expect that people will perform if you are only giving them a pay cheque; give them more meaningful incentives such as professional growth.
    b. Treat people the same; remember they are individuals with different needs and goals.
    c. Pretend that something bad isn't happening; be transparent and welcome expressions of emotion.

Case study 1: Take care of your team

For thirteen years, a friend of one of the authors worked as a recruiter at a staffing firm in the City of London. He managed a small sales force and a temporary staffing division and he loved his job. "The company came first for me. I was a loyal and trusted employee," he says. However, soon after the economic crisis in 2008, the company struggled to maintain its hiring fees and retain clients. Senior leaders decided to cut salaries in the hopes of keeping the operation afloat. They looked for a company that could possibly acquire them.

During this crisis, he took a transparent and supportive approach with his team. "Honesty was the only way to live and work through it," he says. He told his team everything he knew and did his best to support them. He spent time listening to their fears and trying to give them confidence and comfort. "I wanted them to feel good about themselves and the work they had to do every day," he says. To keep them motivated, he was clear that he was living through the same thing. "We were all in the same boat and the people I worked with wanted to know that I was right there with them through fears and all," he says.

As a manager, he felt compelled to take care of his team. "I had a deep and sincere obligation to be useful and to know what they thought, felt, and wanted to do in this emergency," he says. He focused on the facts that he thought would help them stay engaged; the company delivered a product that was well respected in the marketplace; the owner had always looked out for his employees; and the organization had survived difficult times in the past.

Despite all best efforts, however, the office did eventually close. Our friend and his team members were lucky. "We were fortunate, even in a tough job market, to transition into work pretty quickly," he says. Many, including him, were able to find jobs that better suited them. "That is one of the positive things that came out of the situation; people were clear about what they did and did not want to do," he says.

Case study 2: Create an "us vs. the world" attitude

Another good friend of ours was managing a global team of 100 people when sales at the company started declining. He says the business, which sold products to companies in the Tech and Media space, had lost touch with its customers and had ignored important changes in the way they made purchases. When it became clear that the company was in real trouble, he spent time with each person on his team explaining the situation and determining who might be incapable of handling the ambiguity. "Some people don't cope well with uncertainty," he says, so he helped those people find new roles outside of the company.

For the people who stayed, he cultivated an "us vs. the world" attitude. He explained that this was an unprecedented challenge for the company and that they would not be able to succeed without all of them. "The objective of the group was to prove everyone wrong and show that we could save this thing," he says. He focused his team's attention on the near-term and encouraged them to accomplish specific tasks in small, manageable chunks. To ensure momentum, he celebrated even smaller successes and rewarded every job well done. When he spoke with members of his team, he conveyed a message: "Anything is possible, no matter how grim the situation, with the right skills, and with a team ready to fight for each other."

The company was able to survive by getting rid of one part of the company and acquiring a new business unit. "Last year, the business had a record year, which shows that you can make it work with a "no regrets attitude," he says.

Chapter 20: Critical Threats that May Sink Your Business

You are up and running, clients love you, and revenue is growing and only the sky is the limit. These are heady times and we encourage you to savour every victory. While many start-ups are struggling to gain momentum, yours is going gangbusters and growth looks certain and sustainable. All you have got to do is keep doing what you are doing today and profits will start rolling in. Right? Wrong!

A close friend of ours looked at failures in small businesses and the results were shocking. Even when the vital signs look great, three common problems can kill your business just as you are thinking about scaling it up.

1. Is Cash Flow Your Ticking Time Bomb?

About 60% of the businesses she reviewed were profitable when they failed, but they were upside down in terms of cash flow. What does that mean for you? Simply put, profits don't pay the bills ... until you collect your receivables.

You will incur the costs of expansion months before you reap the rewards. If your cash flow doesn't let you cover essential payments to employees, suppliers and the tax man, it's Game Over!

Before you take on huge new sales, invest in capital items, or hire new employees, you need a solid cash flow projection. With this information in hand, you can make an informed decision about planned growth and managing the risks you face.

2. Is Your Business Model Crushing Productivity?

Most people are all fired up about what their businesses do and not so hot on planning process improvements, managing cash flow or even learning to be good leaders. Successful entrepreneurs don't just stumble into profitable growth or at least not that often.

Does your business model support how you want things to run. It makes the difference between focusing your talent where you find satisfaction and reward or racing around putting out fires.

Business models align with the way you deliver value to your customers. For example, if your goal is to be the lowest cost provider of men's briefs (just to pick a vivid idea of a product that the 3 of us use every day) your business model might entail sourcing inventory directly from the manufacturer and selling through low-cost, high-volume marketing channels. Everything you do in this example should improve efficiency, and reduce costs.

3. Is Your Leadership Style Limiting Your Leverage?

Let's say you are a strong extrovert, with a passion for new things and connecting with people, a classic profile for entrepreneurs, and an important aspect of your drive to get things rolling however, you are probably easily frustrated with the detail guys who sweat the risks associated with change. If you are missing out on the value of diverse styles, failure to establish common ground is a common culprit; before you get bent out of shape about your differences, make sure you establish a clear and common purpose; the big WHY as we call it. When you all have the same goal in mind, many of the friction points get easier, or vanish entirely.

Will Your Business Outperform the Odds?

The best piece of advice we have personally ever received is to work **on** your business just as hard as you work ***in*** your business.

Saying you don't know how, or you don't have time, just doesn't cut it. We admire the necessary drive and guts to start a business; but if you want to be successful over the long haul, you need to get curious about what you don't know. Find someone you really admire and discover how they became successful and then shamelessly copy them. Surround yourself with talent, so you have the capacity to become brilliant doing something you love, and reaping the rewards that accompany it. Last but not least keep your high level of integrity and ethics. Don't do any short cuts that you will later bitterly regret. Many sinking Titanics of the business world went down because they lost a basic understanding of business ethics.

Chapter 21: Turning the Titanic

One of the authors had a conversation with a former colleague about culture change recently. We were discussing the much overused phrase "turning the Titanic" as it applies to changing organizational culture.

So many people seem to believe that it's too hard and too slow to make a meaningful change in culture of their organizations. Some managers focus instead on more policies, more process, more red tape and more rules. Others just resign themselves to the current situation.

We would like to challenge that belief. We all know great leaders who have created highly engaged teams within organizations that have less than stellar cultures. What are some of the things they are doing right?

1. **Leaders constantly communicate a compelling view of the culture.**

Why is this a great place to work? Is the team great at identifying and capitalizing on future trends? Is it a flexible environment that allows work life balance? Is it a place where team members can grow their individual careers?

Leaders who are creating a culture are intentional about how they talk about their organization. Sometimes, these conversations are a bit aspirational. That is OKAY. Get the conversation started and move the organization forward towards achieving a mutual goal.

2. **Leaders model and embody the culture making it tangible to everyone.**

Let us give you a real life example of how it doesn't work. In a team where "trust" was listed as a core value, a front line supervisor asked her team to provide a doctor's note if they missed a day of work. The organizational policy was that a doctor's note was required after a 3-day of absence. Do you think there was a culture of trust in this team? The people in your team, in your organization, really are watching you. If you tell them that it is important to innovate, you should be out there taking smart business risks. You should help them navigate the political environment to get some of their innovative ideas implemented. You should also accept that some of them eventually will fail.

3. Leaders hire people with personal values aligned to the culture.

These leaders identify the values that are critical to the success of their team and integrate those values into their hiring process. Think about a company that deploys large cross functional teams to implement new IT systems. It is critical to leaders in that business to find candidates with great technical skills. It is just as important to hire people who demonstrate teamwork capabilities. So a successful leader will interview for technical skills and teamwork at the same time. Maybe she will ask about experiences where the candidate has been a member of a team that has had to work together to reach a common goal or how they approach goals where they have a lot of cross functional dependencies. The candidate will need to demonstrate both the technical skills and values alignment to get an offer.

Are you trying to build a high performing culture in your team or in your organization? What are you doing to turn the Titanic? It didn't actually sneak up on you did it? Looking in the back mirror you knew it was happening the whole time. You just didn't know how bad it really was because you were afraid to face the music. But one day you woke up and realized your team and your organisation had spiralled out of control. What now?

Steering wheel on a wooden boat.

We will use the analogy of someone trying to lose weight. It can be like you are driving the Titanic the wrong way and you need to turn it a full 180 degrees. You know it's possible and that you should do it but the thought of how long it will take and all the work required to make it happen keeps you from turning that wheel.

The problem is you are focused on the big picture. All you can think about is all the weight you need to lose. All the exercise you will need to do. All the food you will need to give up. All the friends that will harp on you for being selfish (trust us, it will happen). All the sacrifices you will have to make and all the time it will take to turn this ship.

It's paralyzing isn't it?

We are not saying you shouldn't know what the end goal, the big picture, is. It is absolutely necessary to have a very clear idea of what it is and more importantly, why it is relevant to you. Meaning how is achieving this goal going to improve your life? Remember, a goal without a reason for accomplishing it is just a dream or a wish.

The main reason for having a goal is not for motivation, it's to give you a target. It's your bull's-eye. Imagine throwing darts without a bull's-eye! What would be the point? Just to throw darts to see what you can hit? Oh wait, that doesn't work because you should still be aiming for something. We guess there is no point of throwing darts with nothing to aim at. Such as there really is no reason to exercise unless you know what you are aiming for. Your goal provides direction and gives your workouts a purpose.

What you need to do is think smaller!

That is right, think smaller. Let us ask you this, if you had to choose between swimming across the ocean or swimming across a pond what would rather do? Swim across the pond right? Why? Because it's easier! You are confident you could cross the pond. The ocean? Not so much.

What about running a marathon? You don't just get up off the couch and run 26 miles right? Of course not! That would be impossible, not to mention it would be really stupid. Instead, you would do the smart thing and starts running short distances and build up to a marathon. You need to take the same approach to getting yourself or your organisation back in shape.

Here are our four suggested steps to turning your Titanic around:

1. **Identify the big goal:** Although you won't stay focused on this it does provide you direction of where you want to go and what you want to accomplish.

2. **Ask yourself why you want to achieve your goal:** This is very important as it's your motivation and the reason why you want to

reach your goal. In other words, what does this goal represent to you? The answer to that question must spark an emotion and light a fire within you.

3. **Determine your first step:** Find just one thing you can do to get the process started. Walk 15 minutes every day for a week for example. Once you have accomplished that, you can build on it by adding another action step.

4. **Forget about the big picture and stay focused on each individual step:** Once you have set the goal and determined your action steps, forget about it and focus only on completing the action steps. Before you know it, you will have reached your goal!

Remember, you are the one driving the Titanic the wrong direction. It doesn't turn the same way a car does. It takes time…a lot of time. It takes effort…a lot of effort. It takes dedication…a lot of dedication. It takes pain…a lot of pain. You get our point yet? It's going to take a lot of a lot of things.

So stop focusing on everything it is going to take and focus on the things you know you can do. Like turning the wheel and you will finally reach the harbour you aimed for.

Chapter 22: How Small Businesses Can Keep Their Ship from Sinking

No one goes into business to fail, but it is an all-too-often occurrence to see a business set sail and quickly sink. Once a business falls into a financial pitfall, it can be hard for the business to climb out. However, knowing what potentially can cause your business to sink and taking precautions to avoid the collapse can not only save your business, but help it to thrive.

Based on personal experiences of the authors, here are some tips on what you can do to help avoid a sinking ship.

1. Do Proper Research

You don't know what you don't know until you learn it. Many failing businesses lack the drive to do research into all aspects of their business. They underestimate staffing needs, pick a bad location or lack the knowledge of what their competitors are doing. Having a great product or idea doesn't always mean success. Before jumping into a project, do your research and form your business plan off what you discover. There are many free to low-cost resources out there to help you succeed. You don't need to involve an expensive consultant; keep it simple.

2. Financial Management

Don't try to do it all. Focus on what your goal is; your business. Hire good people to help you succeed. You should always know exactly where your business stands so that you can always make quick and important business decisions.

3. Never Stop Learning

Part of your success will be what you know and how you continue to learn about your business. Look to local universities or resources who offer business advising services or classes on financial management courses. Also, learn as much as you can about your business. Key areas to focus on are legal matters related to your business, contracting, marketing, technology and finances.

4. Build Business Credit

Keeping your business credit and your personal credit separate is important. Anything you purchase for the business should be under your business entity to help protect you personally. You can always be the guarantor to help support the credit for the company in the beginning.

To maintain a successful company, your work is never done. Most start-ups fail within three years. Failure occurs when the market turns and they are no longer able to compete or they have simply not built enough credit to allow themselves to grow. Stay tuned into your financials and never stop learning and adapting.

With those key takeaways, your business will be on the road to many years of success.

5. Time is Money

We all know time is money and the captain is responsible for the ship. As the business owner, you are the captain of the ship. Do not worry. Feeling stuck is common and so is the feeling of wanting to throw in the towel, especially during this challenging economy of today. Before you drown, let us throw you a life preserver. The purpose of a business is to earn money. If your business is not earning you money, then it is a costly, time-consuming hobby. In order to be profitable, you have to make more money than it costs to operate your business. This is simple but often times we forget the first rule of business and get distracted with everything else such as organizing our desks, ordering supplies, doing research, having meetings, running errands, talking on the phone and surfing the internet.

Out of respect for time and money, we have compiled five ideas you can implement to start enjoying and profiting from your business.

1. We have discovered that most times, our **mindset** is the reason for feeling stuck. We are limited by our beliefs. If you do not believe, you will not try to make things happen. See the possibilities and start believing it can happen.

If you do not see your business as the vessel to take you on the journey you desire, you will not fuel nor navigate the ship. The fuel is the energy and resources required to get the engine started.

Remind yourself by writing down why you are in business in the first place. See your business as enjoyable and allow yourself to be passionate about it. This way you will see it with new eyes. If you cannot see yourself engaging in your business in a joyful way, you may lose interest. Be sure there are no external factors affecting your ability to see beyond the current crisis.

Remember your mindset is infectious. Your employees, customers and loved ones will view your business as you do. Develop what we call a "Brick Mindset" A Brick Mindset holds you accountable to put forth the effort you need to get the maximum return on your time and investment.

2. Remember, **self-employed is not unemployed**! Often times, people see business owners, especially those who work from home as unemployed. These people do not understand that you have a job and without it, you cannot pay your bills or put food on the table.

Now, we must caution you. As one of the authors said "Sometimes it is not just other people. We too forget that we are employed and are responsible for the success and failure of our business".

Knowing how to manage your time, prioritizing business responsibilities from your personal ones is critical. You need set business hours and a list of things to accomplish that all lead to your purpose of being in business to earn a profit. Laundry, getting the car washed and all the other distractions including taking the day off when business needs to be done is not acceptable.

Ask yourself, would you hire you? If the answer is no then fire yourself. Then sit down, write out in complete details what the responsibilities are of the new employee and rehire yourself to do the job correctly this time. If you cannot do the job, perhaps you need to hire someone who can or outsource the functions you are not able to perform.

3. The solution to number 2 above can be found in the old and still relevant adage,

"If you fail to plan, plan to fail!"

Most people are not operating their businesses like a business. They are treating it like a hobby. Businesses make money and require focus, planning and action. If you do not manage your time and are not following a plan, you will feel like "A chicken running around without a head."

You do not need to write out an entire business plan, though it will be a great help if you do so. At minimum, you need to identify what your business does and who your customers are. Then determine how you are going to make them aware you exist and how you are going to convince them to do business with you.

You will also need to plan your daily, weekly and monthly activities. If possible, plan even longer to make sure that everything you do is consistent with your mission and your purpose.

Make your list of priorities for the next day immediately at the close of business. Do not wait until later or in the morning, write it down while you are in the work mode.

A business needs a written plan to maintain structure. Not having structure is a sure way to destroy your business. Treat your business seriously because it is serious. If it is not, then it is a hobby.

4. If you have not heard or discovered it on your own, **multitasking is not very effective**. There are some things that can be grouped together but make sure you do not combine menial tasks with income generating activities. Income generating activities, as do most things, require your undivided attention. Multitasking slows you down and causes you to make mistakes.

It is best to focus on the most important activities first. Then move onto the urgent tasks. Do not, we repeat, do not start with the easiest or most enjoyable activities. Those are usually the least productive and do nothing to make you money or build your client list.

Being busy is not the same as being productive and long hours do not necessarily translate into more profits. Sometimes the best thing you can do for your business is to take a break. If necessary, network with people who are serious about their business and learn by asking questions and observing how they operate their businesses.

5. Without promotion something terrible happens... Nothing!

To grow your business you have to get busy, get out and get the word out. Give them something to talk about and they will help you to spread the word!

Sometimes, you may need to upgrade the look and content of your website and promotional materials. Your potential customers may not be responding to your offer because they maybe judging your book or business by its cover.

If your business cards, flyers, website and other promotional materials do not look fresh and appealing, then you are not going to keep your potential customers attention long enough for them to buy. Try testing a different style of business cards and different colours on your website and materials.

You may need to develop a blog, create a Facebook fan page, open an Instagram account to promote your images, make use of YouTube, LinkedIn and Twitter. In fact, there are hundreds of free internet based services for you to take advantage.

Do not forget off-line marketing as well. Chambers of Commerce, breakfast clubs, mixers, local community based organizations, charitable events and political networking opportunities.

Do not forget the media. Local radio, television and print media are always interested in a good story to help their audiences. If you want to establish yourself as an expert in your field and potentially earn a nice living, you can even write articles as well as publish a book.

As a business owner, you want to avoid capsizing. So here are five lessons you can learn from the Titanic's fate:

1. Keep your eyes on the Horizon: The Titanic's crew failed to keep a sharp lookout for icebergs, a bad idea given how difficult it is to quickly turn a huge cruise liner. This was their fatal error, as icebergs turned out to be in unusual places that year. New research reveals the reason why an unusually close moon caused an exceptionally high tide, moving icebergs that would ordinarily stay near shore out into deep water, and into Titanic's path.

This news reminds us of what happened in industries such as video-rentals and the music business; old-school companies continued on the usual course and ignored all signs that the marketplace had changed to a digital realm. The result was that new competitors stole their customers while older businesses floundered. Stay alert to new trends and a changing marketplace to make sure your business does not go down.

2. Don't Become Arrogant: Titanic was famously promoted as being "unsinkable." No business should ever think of itself as invulnerable. Few businesses last forever, and they all have weaknesses. Smart business owners reduce the dangers by considering and planning for every possible risk even those that seem almost unimaginable.

3. Plan for problems: The Titanic sinking would be known as far less of a tragedy if the ship had been equipped with enough lifeboats. According to RMS Titanic Inc., whose mission is to preserve the Titanic's artefacts and history, the ship complied with then-current law, which didn't account for a vessel of Titanic's size. Instead of doing the right thing, Titanic's builders cut corners to preserve deck space and cut costs.

But the real cost of this casual attitude toward safety was the loss of more than 1,500 lives. Hopefully your business mistakes won't cause deaths, but if yours operates any sort of physical plant, be sure to practice evacuation drills with employees. Make sure fire alarms and exits are all operational.

4. Don't neglect training: The Titanic's evacuation was delayed by lack of crew and passenger training and preparation. There was no lifeboat drill once Titanic sailed and lifeboats turned out to be less than fully provisioned. The result was chaos and confusion, and likely fewer lives saved. The best company in the world can't run properly if employees don't know what to do and how to do it.

5. Worry about the important stuff: The term "rearranging deck chairs on the Titanic" has come to symbolize an inappropriate focus on the small stuff when there are big, underlying problems. This is something we have seen too many business owners do. If the ship is sinking, get down to the engine room and find out why.

Chapter 23: Ways to Save Your Sinking Company

Sometimes companies find themselves on the wrong track. Whether due to flawed strategy, incompetent management or even a handful of small glitches that slow down the entire enterprise; some businesses just need someone to come in and make big decisions to change course.

One of the authors spent some time with a turnaround CEO recently to talk about some of his turnaround experiences and what he learned from them. Below are the 7 key learnings.

1. Eliminate Preconceived Notions and Become a Blank Slate

He said "When you are first looking at a business or getting familiar with a business, you hear a lot from the founders or other co-workers or the news about what their problems are, what their issues are or what they need to do. I find that people often will analyze a business and provide the answers or the solutions without ever really knowing the business intimately. If you drown out the noise, the secret to a company's woes are easier to hear."

2. Focus on the People

"So many people make the mistake of looking at the software, looking at the hardware, looking at their reports, looking at all of the assets and not the most important asset initially, which is human capital; the human asset. All of those systems, procedures and protocols are only as good as the people driving them and that is infinitely more important."

Though common wisdom may show some personnel to be stars and others to be mediocre, he said he found such assumptions to be false, pointing to his first rule of approaching an ailing company with an open mind because all of the internal employees and managers have some kind of agenda.

"When I was at one the companies I was brought in to turnaround, initially I was looking at one of their divisions. I kept hearing all the way from HR to a corporate VP and some other people about this one senior sales person who was just a superstar and how this whole division would be at a loss without this one guy who singlehandedly was doing 25% of the business. That didn't sit well with me because that shows me a flaw/problems with procedure. I didn't let the opinions taint my process."

Upon closer analysis, the superstar in question, he says, turned out to be cannibalizing business to the detriment of his co-workers. "Within weeks of letting this person go, four or five other people increased their numbers dramatically and overall the results of the company were much better than before."

3. Act Fast But Don't Act Stupid

When quick changes need to be made to turn around a suffering company, those changes could be penny-wise and pound foolish. "Axing this process or this vendor or this product or compromising the quality of the product for one that is inferior will lead to an initial cost savings but in the long run could ensure that your business further deteriorates." In other words, avoid going into panic mode.

4. Do Not Hide From The Truth

When you are planning a turnaround mission you have to be realistic about the timeline you give yourself to figure out if your plans are working and the business is indeed turning around. If you are not realistic about the problems facing the company, your timeline will be off and your new strategy will be flawed. He found himself faced with such miscommunication at one of his turnaround projects.

He said "The board of directors and the outgoing CEO at the time didn't fully clue me in on the severity of their problems, and what I knew of them was pretty severe. My first day there I learned it was much deeper than anyone had cared to share and they were on the verge of just simply shutting the doors there or going into bankruptcy." The company owed product to a million of customers; some who had been waiting for six months for delivery; but didn't have the capital to manufacture let alone deliver product. "I started the reorganization the day I started." After cuts to payroll, utility, scheduling reorganization and talking to vendors and creditors, the company was able to pull through.

5. Remember, a CEO Should Calm Nerves, Not Amplify Anxiety

Being secretive, evasive and opaque is a good way to turn up the volume on the rumours and whispers employees are already generating. "When the senior team is sneaking in and out of the office or holding secret closed-door meetings or saying one thing to one group and another thing to another that is just increases the acceleration to which the business declines."

6. Don't Be Driven By Pride Or Fear

Fear can make you do foolish things, especially when trying to resuscitate an ailing business. When things are going wrong, fingers get pointed. Too often CEOs or top managers have too much pride to admit their mistakes and the entire organization suffers for it. Their stubborn nature can be a hole in the bow of a sinking ship. "For me it's one of the criteria I use to determine whether I'm going to work with a business or not," he said. "If I see that the owner or CEO is very belligerent and half the lights are off in his building and he hasn't drawn a pay cheque in a while yet he seems unable or unwilling to truly change, that is a huge mistake."

But sometimes inability to change stems from fear, not pride. "It's easier to dump a CRM or a manufacturing vendor than it is to let go of the person in the office next to them, or upstairs or downstairs, or to hire somebody that is more knowledgeable and experienced than they themselves are."

7. Allow People a Chance to Turn Themselves Around for the Good of the Company (Cut Them Loose If They Don't)

In a turnaround mission, he says that when he sees a manager or employee behaving in a way that is not in step with the company's corporate culture and values, he will take them aside and tell them in a warm and friendly manner that their way of thinking cannot continue. "This is the situation that we are in, this is how you have chosen to respond to this situation and these are the ramifications of your actions and then just to hit it home I will repeat it; you did this and the end result is this, and it has magnified this problem."

Unfortunately, some people have a hard time changing with the tides. "I talked to a VP about making the situation they were in better instead of worse and he was crying," he said. "He told me he got it. As I was leaving, I was going to shake his hand and he wanted to give me a hug." But the change he was hoping for in the manager did not quite happen. "Sure enough, two hours later, the same action," he remembers. "This company did not have the luxury of time to teach this person how to be an ethical person, how to be a good businessman, how to be part of the team that was going to rebuild the infrastructure, not dismantle it. So I let him go."

Chapter 24: When the Ship is Sinking

Many companies falter, and some will fail. How you lead your ship through the storm can make all the difference.

Thanks to the Great Recession, we happen to know three businesses that are currently on the way out.

All three were stunningly profitable in 2008. But now, all three are losing money. All three have a business model that is probably past its prime. Not one is paying the owners any salary at all.

Despite these similarities, the owners of these companies have very different perspectives on how to handle impending failure. One is frantically bailing. One is paddling as hard as he can and one is preparing for a long solo swim.

1. Bail faster

If the ship is taking on water or the company is losing money most managers' first reaction is to cut costs. Throw the deadweight overboard. Bail out the water with every available bucket. In a large measure, these entrepreneurs are smart, forward thinking, and it's likely that they will survive the recession.

But where will they be when it's all over? Probably in the same place.

If you put effort into bailing, you are not pushing forward, and you are not making progress. In the end, you are a smaller ship, just as far from shore, but with less manpower to move you closer to your goal. Is the original goal so important that you put all your effort into cost-cutting and downsizing?

2. Paddle harder

If cutting costs does not come naturally, the temptation is to chart a path around the storm and paddle harder in a new direction. When the market is shrinking, don't give up just change course and work hard to make progress. The good news is you might feel the wind in your hair. You are moving - going somewhere.

But a new direction takes you into uncharted waters. You have no experience in the new markets you are entering, and no understanding of the perils ahead.

Are you really any better off? It's easy to get that sinking feeling all over again.

3. Swim for it

The third option is to abandon ship. When irons turns to broach, even the best captain wonders whether he is doomed to go down with his ship. An experienced entrepreneur hears the siren call of new adventures and might just decide to jump overboard and swim for shore.

But when a company leader calls it quits; closes the doors and sends the crew packing; who benefits? Not the crew. Not the customers and not the captain who was counting on equity to buy his retirement yacht.

Still, the prospect of cutting losses can sound better than the forecast of continued stalls or squalls. Bailing out can be a lot easier than bailing water.

The swimmer we know seems prepared to go it alone maybe even to sit out the storm and do very little until better weather stirs him back to the entrepreneurial seas.

Lessons learned. The recession continues to hamper all kinds of businesses and if it's not the recession, then it's changes in technology, in consumer spending, or in government regulation. Eventually, all businesses face the perfect storm —sooner or later.

So prepare now. When your ship takes on water, are you going to bail, paddle, or swim?

It is not over till it's over!

Our suggestion is for you to save your failing business. If your life's dream is in trouble cheer up as we look at the techniques experience entrepreneurs and new owners use to restore failing businesses.

If your creditors and the IRS in the US and Inland Revenue in the UK are nipping at your heels, instead of feeling sorry for yourself, fretting, and worrying about the troubles you are facing, give yourself a new job. First, fire yourself as president; after all, you did create the problems you now must solve. Next, put on a new hat and appoint yourself to the newly created position of "Consultant and Turnaround Specialist." Before you start to say this is a ridiculous idea, think about it this way. If you were presented with the opportunity to take over a troubled business such as yours, what would you do? Would you not find a way to restore it to health with a positive attitude and action? Of course you would, it would be foolish to pass up such an opportunity now do it for your financial future.

There is no mystery to putting a troubled company back on the path to success. If your customers are still there and your product or service is not obsolete, most likely you can taste prosperity again. The "pros" that grab near defunct businesses and restore them to health, will tell you to:

1. Cut out every unnecessary expense and regardless of the pain; reduce all expenses.

2. Be a miser with cash. Grab every dime owed to you and delay paying your bills as long as possible without creating more problems for yourself.

3. Increase sales - start selling your products and services the way you did when you started the company.

We write from the pain of personal experience. In April 2010, one of the companies one of the authors use to work for was facing collapse from, debt, declining sales, and a severe cash shortage. They closed the manufacturing plant, sold the equipment to pay some of the debt and arranged with a subcontractor to do the manufacturing and moved the remains of the company to a small office suite.

The suppliers were suing for payment and they were barely able to pay the telephone bill and the office rent. The company was broke. They dreaded the mail, especially those certified letters; they knew they did not contain good news. They dreaded the phone calls as irate creditors are not always polite. They could not even declare bankruptcy, as they did not have money to pay the attorney.

They desperately sought a solution. As they could not pay the bills and the new subcontractor insisted on controlling the accounts receivable (keeping most of the receipts), they were left with the only option of going on the road selling. It helped. They were now able to pick up enough business to cover the telephone and rent, but little was left to pay the debts.

Eventually, creditors grew tired of their promises and sued obtaining judgments. As they were unable to pay anyone anything and with no money for a lawyer, they accepted these dreaded court documents not knowing what to do.

All of their previous business experience and education did not prepare them for these emotions of failure. As former executives and business school MBA holders, they were not setting an example of successful entrepreneurship. The feelings of self-confidence and self-worth evaporated. In a year, they went from the excitement of a new business to desperation. It was awful.

In this example they had to learn it the hard way how to save the business and they did. YOU can do the same.

Chapter 25: Unsung Heroes of Business World

We cannot conclude this book without acknowledging all of the unsung heroes who have changed the business world and yet, we do not know of their efforts. Throughout history, people have changed the business world seeking neither reward nor recognition. Therefore we believe these acts of conscience and courage should be acknowledged and celebrated, and thus commit us to discovering and sharing these remarkable stories.

Over 100 years after the sinking of the Titanic among the disproportionate number of men who perished largely due to the ship's "women and children first" emergency protocol only two are said to be black; Joseph Laroche, 26, a Haitian-born, French-educated engineer who was moving back to Haiti because he could not find work in his profession; and Victor Giglio, the son of an Italian father and Egyptian mother, and personal secretary to U.S. industrialist Benjamin Guggenheim.

Giglio and Laroche are actually believed to be the only men of colour aboard the ill-fated ship, which carried 2,224 people on its route to New York.

According to the Chicago Tribune, who talked with a descendent of Laroche, the engineer and his family were never meant to board the Titanic to begin with.

Laroche's mother had sent the family first-class tickets to travel on the French liner France. But just before departure, the Laroches learned that the ship wouldn't allow them to dine with their children. Out of concern about the younger daughter, who was sickly, they traded their tickets for second-class tickets on the Titanic.

Laroche's pregnant wife, Juliette, 22, and their two daughters made it off the ship and are said to have returned to France, where they lived in poverty for a few years until Juliette won a settlement from the Titanic disaster.

Laroche, however, did not, sharing the same fate as Victor Giglio, who stoically sat sipping brandy with his boss, declaring they were "prepared to go down like gentlemen," the Daily Mail reports.

An archivist at Ampleforth, the North Yorkshire boarding school Giglio attended, recently unearthed a photo taken 11 years before he died on the Titanic.

Though he was favoured by Guggenheim, travelling first class, unlike Guggenheim's chauffeur, who died in second class, according to John Graves, Curator of Ship History at the National Maritime Museum in Greenwich, South East London, it is likely that Giglio would have been denied a lifeboat because of his skin colour.

Giglio and Laroche's stories add another little-known facet to the Titanic's tragic tale, which is being retold with the re-release of James Cameron's 1997 film and through a memorial cruise scheduled to visit the wreckage site.

We should not forget any of our modern day's unsung business heroes all over the world just the way both Giglio and Laroche's stories was never told whenever we have seen the Titanic's tragic tale.

We should remember that an unsung hero is a role model whose generous acts of compassion, strength, selflessness, perseverance and, quite possibly, sacrifice make a profound and positive difference on the course of history. It is those unsung heroes that very often keep our businesses afloat.

Chapter 26: Concluding the Journey

In our opinion here are three of the main factors that led to the sinking of the unsinkable Titanic.

1. First, the captain and navigator didn't heed iceberg warnings because they believed the ship to be unsinkable. The Titanic had been built with twelve specially-designed compartments below deck. The idea was that if the ship hit an iceberg, the compartment with the hole would contain the incoming water. However, if more than four compartments were compromised, the ship would sink. No one ever imagined that such a scenario could happen. But when Titanic struck the iceberg, five compartments were filled with water, rendering her incapable to staying afloat. The Titanic was supposed to be unsinkable. Unrealistic self-confidence and complacency led to the unimaginable tragedy; just like the too big to fail corporations all over the world!

2. Second, poor planning further contributed to the death of many of the Titanic's passengers. Only 20 lifeboats were on board; not nearly enough to hold all the passengers. Lack of lifeboats was mainly due to aesthetics; the designers wanted to keep the first class deck clear of ugly lifeboats. Ironically, first class

passengers were much more likely to survive; the second and third class passengers drowned because the wealthy wanted to be able to sip cocktails with an unobstructed view. Arrogance led to needless deaths; many more passengers would have been saved had there been sufficient lifeboats.

3. Finally, disorganization and lack of training created chaos on board of the Titanic between the time of the iceberg strike and the sinking. The captain originally failed to call for evacuation, because he thought the leak could be contained. But once he called for the crew to begin putting passengers into lifeboats, another problem emerged. The crew had not been properly trained about evacuation procedures. They weren't sure how many people would fit in each boat, so they underfilled the lifeboats. Most boats were launched only half full. There were also problems releasing the lifeboats and some got tangled up as they were lowered to the sea. Lack of training led to a disorganized evacuation that wasn't as effective as it could and should have been.

The impact of the sinking of the Titanic was felt all over the world and continues to be a historical event of note. Important lessons were learned about safety equipment, training and engineering. But those lessons faded after time. Nearly 100 years later, the Costa Concordia sank, resulting in the deaths of 30 people (two people are still missing and considered dead as well). The captain of the Concordia was also overly self-confident, irresponsible, arrogant and complacent. He wanted to impress his wealthy passengers, so he navigated too close to the coastline and ran aground, tearing a huge gash in the hull of the ship. Concorida's captain, like the captain of the Titanic, also failed to evacuate passengers quickly. The crew was unprepared to perform evacuation, an unfortunate similarity of the Titanic.

What can business practitioners learn from these two tragedies?

Here are a few tips

1. No business is unsinkable or too big to fail. Even companies with long histories and market share can fail (remember Lehman Brothers?) Don't get complacent with your business. Take time to build a business plan that includes all contingencies, including sinking (figuratively, not literally!) and make sure that your designs are solid.

2. Extreme self-confidence and arrogance lead to even greater downfall. Admit mistakes early in order to salvage your business.

3. Unless your business relies solely on wealthy customers, make policies based on everyone's needs.

4. Stick to the basics; keep up with current standards and practices. The Costa Concordia didn't bother to have a safety drill, so passengers and crew didn't know what to do.

5. Give employees the power to make decisions. If they see that something is wrong, they should be able to take action. On both the Titanic and the Costa Concordia crew members stood around waiting for instructions when they clearly needed to be evacuating passengers.

6. There is no guarantee that you can keep your business from experiencing a disaster.

Sometimes bad things do happen. What you can do is to plan and prepare properly, so that if you hit an iceberg, run aground or just have a sales slump, you are ready. It all starts with realizing that there may be challenging icebergs ahead although you can't see them.

Simply put: Keep Your Eyes On the Horizon and Avoid Sinking!

Other Book from the same Authors

You can get a copy of Paperback, Kindle and Audio Version of this book from Amazon.com, iTunes Store and any other major book stores including University Libraries worldwide.

www.ingramcontent.com/pod-product-compliance
Lightning Source LLC
Chambersburg PA
CBHW071424170526
45165CB00001B/384